Don't Steal Copyrighted Stuff!

Avoiding Plagiarism and Illegal Internet Downloading

Ann Graham Gaines

Enslow Publishers, Inc.
40 Industrial Road
Box 398
Berkeley Heights, NJ 07922
USA

http://www.enslow.com

Library of Congress Cataloging-in-Publication Data

Gaines, Ann.
  Don't steal copyrighted stuff! : avoiding plagiarism and illegal internet downloading / Ann Graham Gaines.
      p. cm.
  Summary: "Learn how to research and write reports with proper citations and bibliographies. Also find out how to protect your own creative works"—Provided by publisher.
  Includes bibliographical references and index.
  ISBN-13: 978-0-7660-2861-6 (alk. paper)
  ISBN-10: 0-7660-2861-5 (alk. paper)
1. Plagiarism. 2. Bibliographical citations. 3. Downloading of data.
4. Copyright infringement. I. Title.
  PN167.G35 2008
  808—dc22

                                    2007008370

Printed in the United States of America

10 9 8 7 6 5 4 3 2 1

To Our Readers:
We have done our best to make sure that all Internet Addresses in this book were active and appropriate when we went to press. However, the author and publisher have no control over and assume no liability for the material available on those Internet sites or on other Web sites they may link to. Any comments or suggestions can be sent by e-mail to comments@enslow.com or to the address on the back cover.

Cover Photo: © Comstock/Corbis. **Interior Photos:** Acclaim Images/Verna Bice, p. 49; Acclaim Images/Felipe Rodriguez, p. 69; Acclaim Images/Mary-Ella Keith, p. 109; Alamy/Visual Arts Library (London), p. 96; Associated Press, p. 31; AP/Chitose Suzuki, p. 5; AP/John S. Stewart, p. 174; AP/Cheryl Gerber, p. 12; AP/Rich Pedroncelli, p. 167; AP/Bruce Lee, p. 131; AP/Greg Swiercz, p.103; AP/Paul Sakuma, p. 123; Christine Balderas, pp. 71, 74, 76; Getty Images/Joe Raedle, p. 8; Getty Images/Robert Sullivan, p. 44; iStockphoto.com/Dovile Butvilaite, pp. 72, 73, 74, 164; iStockphoto.com/Rarpia, p. 2, 159.

Contents

In the News

IN APRIL OF 2006, KAAVYA VISWANATHAN seemed to have it all. At the age of nineteen, the Indian-American woman was in her second year at Harvard University. When she graduated, she wanted to become an investment banker. But in the meantime, she had begun what seemed certain to be a successful career as a writer.

Born in India, Kaavya Viswanathan came to the United States as a child. Her parents, both doctors, always provided her with a very comfortable life. She went to one of the best high schools in New Jersey and believed that she would probably get to go to a great college. During the summers, she went to camps with other talented kids from wealthy families, and during the school year, she was editor of her school newspaper. And she had already written a six-hundred-page novel by the time she was ready to apply to college.

Kaavya Viswanathan at Harvard University in 2006.

When that time came, her parents spent at least $10,000 to have Katherine Cohen, a college admissions counselor, help Viswanathan get into the college of her dreams. They knew Cohen would help their daughter prepare for tests like the SAT and write a great college admissions essay. It was a great surprise when Cohen also helped Viswanathan line up a book deal. Cohen was so impressed by Viswanathan's writing that she put the girl in contact with a literary agent, a professional who helps authors make book deals. As a result, the publisher Little, Brown & Company gave Viswanathan a contract for two books and an advance payment of $500,000. That's right, the teenager received half a million dollars! First-time authors usually get just a fraction of that. Viswanathan was the youngest author Little, Brown & Company had ever signed.

Viswanathan worked with a book packager, or a company that makes books for publishers to sell, to write her first book for Little, Brown & Company. It was titled *How Opal Mehta Got Kissed, Got Wild, and Got a Life.* Even before it hit bookstore shelves in the spring of 2006, it was getting rave reviews. Newspapers such as *The New York Times* ran profiles of Viswanathan. She was invited to appear on the hottest talk shows. DreamWorks, one of the biggest movie production companies in the United States, talked about turning her novel into a movie.[1]

Then, suddenly, Viswanathan's popularity plummeted. On April 23, *The Harvard Crimson,* her college's newspaper, ran a short article that said Viswanathan had been accused of plagiarism. A critic charged that she hadn't written her whole book herself, but had stolen parts of it from another writer. A reader had noticed that, in certain places, Viswanathan's book was very similar to two young adult novels written by another author named Megan McCafferty.[2]

From that point on, the situation got worse and worse for Viswanathan. McCafferty and her publisher, Random House, issued angry statements to the press. Day after day, Viswanathan's name appeared in the news as the charges grew. On April 26, she went on television. She appeared on *The Today Show,* where she told the news anchor Katie Couric that if she had plagiarized, it still wasn't her fault. She declared she hadn't meant to do so. She blamed what she described as her photographic memory.[3] She basically said she remembers everything she reads word for word. With all of this information in her mind, she thought it was possible that she mixed up what were her own ideas and phrasings with words from a book that inspired her. Viswanathan's agent, Jennifer Rudolph Walsh, told a

Then, suddenly, Viswanathan's popularity plummeted.

reporter that "Somewhere in her mind, she crossed an invisible line with this material and didn't realize that the words so easy and available to her were not her own."[4]

Over time, it was shown that Viswanathan's book contained no fewer than forty passages that very closely resembled those in other books. The books were written not just by Megan McCafferty, but by a variety of authors. Viswanathan was raked over the coals by the press. She continued to act as if the charges against her were unfair. Toward the end of the month of May, Little, Brown & Company acknowledged that the problem was extremely serious. The publisher recalled her book—meaning all copies were taken off bookstore shelves—and canceled her contract. Presumably, she was required to return her advance. Because of accusations of plagiarism, Viswanathan experienced public humiliation as well as possibly a huge financial loss. It still remains to be seen what effect this episode will have on the rest of her life.

Similarities were found between Viswanathan's book and works by Megan McCafferty and Sophie Kinsella.

Viswanathan's story is not the only plagiarism case to make news headlines in recent years. There were two other big cases that made the news in 2006 alone. On March 25, 2006, the *Washington Times* reported that researchers in the United States had discovered that parts of a thesis written by Vladimir Putin, the president of Russia, had been plagiarized from a book published in the United States in 1978. The man who discovered the plagiarism—Clifford Gaddy—described Putin as "cutting corners."[5] Two months later, *The New York Times* reported that a famous businessman named William Swanson, chief executive of the Raytheon Company, was being punished by his company. He was going to be paid almost $1 million less than expected for the year because he had plagiarized in a book of rules he had put together for managers.[6]

Duke University's Center for Academic Integrity is one group that says plagiarism is an increasing problem. According to a study the center released in the summer of 2005, almost half of all college students admit to having at some point cheated on a written assignment, like a research paper. They've found the same to be true of high school students. The center says "Internet plagiarism is a growing concern on all campuses as students struggle to understand what constitutes acceptable use of the Internet. . . . A majority of students (77%) believe such cheating is not a very serious issue."[7]

There's also widespread concern about a problem closely related to plagiarism. It's called copyright infringement. Infringement is the word used when someone infringes on—disregards or violates—a certain kind of right. Copyrights are legal rights that apply to creative works, including books, music, and works of art; copyrights are granted to creative people, including authors, composers, and artists. In the United States, copyright law says creators have the right to control how their work is used—whether they write books or make art or record music. The creators are supposed to be able to say when their work can be copied.

Students often break copyright law, usually without realizing it. It happens both when they are working on school assignments and when they are pursuing their own hobbies. Most often, students infringe on copyright when they are downloading material onto a computer. People download music, videos, video games, and software over the Internet. Much of what they do is perfectly legal, such as buying songs from iTunes or an antivirus package from Symantec.

But some students are guilty of illegal downloading. To go online to any site and download copyrighted material of any kind without permission is illegal. According to the law, people are not supposed to trade copyrighted music, software, or videos over the Internet. Many students do this not just at home but at school. As a result, schools have begun to institute strict downloading policies.

American educators regard both plagiarism and illegal downloading of copyrighted materials as extremely serious problems. They want students to understand why both are wrong and how to avoid them. It is important to learn how to fairly and legally use a variety of materials for school projects and when pursuing personal interests.

Chapter 1

What Is Plagiarism?

FROM AN EARLY AGE, students learn they should not copy from other students. As they get older, they learn that it's also against the rules to copy from sources—such as books or articles—that they use without credit in their school projects. To do so is to plagiarize. Throughout their school years, students may receive many warnings against plagiarism. Yet many do not know exactly what plagiarism is. That is understandable. It can be difficult to grasp exactly what is included in the idea of "plagiarism."

What Is Plagiarism, Exactly?

There are many words in the English language that can be defined easily. There's little disagreement as to what a barracuda is. The same holds true for a book or a boogie board. Plagiarism, on the other hand, is very difficult to define. Look up *plagiarize* in a dictionary. It may give a simple definition, talking just about presenting someone else's work as one's own. *Plagiarism* is the term used when one writer copies the words of another. For example, when someone gives a speech and uses someone else's words without saying they're doing so, that's

Teachers consider plagiarism to be a form of cheating.

plagiarism. It is also applied to situations in which an artist or songwriter steals another's material. The list of the types of work that can be plagiarized goes on and on. It includes writings of all sorts: books, magazine and journal articles, newspaper articles, and poems. It also includes speeches, music, art, software, architectural design, movies, video games, and more.

In some cases, definitions of plagiarism also talk about copying someone else's ideas. To some, this doesn't seem right. After all, more than one person can come up with the same idea independently. Also, American copyright law says ideas should be allowed to circulate freely. Most educators would agree with both points. However, they would probably go on to say this: Students do come up with some ideas on their own. But, they also frequently encounter others' ideas while learning. It's important for students to realize that they must acknowledge it, or admit it, when they get an idea from someone else. And that's true not just for people in school but also those in the workplace.

Partly because plagiarism is a hard word to define, it's a subject of great debate. To help students understand the concept better, it is often talked about in school honor codes. In an honor code, a school sets out rules students must follow. These are not the rules that govern behavior in a cafeteria, for example. Rather, they are the rules that have to do with cheating. Schools' honor codes often refer to plagiarism as a form of cheating. At San Diego's Union High School, plagiarism is considered a matter of academic dishonesty.[1] The University of Victoria is one school that specifically calls it cheating.[2]

Other schools are very careful to point out that there's both intentional and unintentional

plagiarism.[3] When they talk about intentional plagiarism, they mean that sometimes people plagiarize
on purpose. For example, they copy an entire paper.
This is an act of deceit. On the other hand, sometimes students plagiarize unintentionally. This means
they do not know they are doing it. This often
happens when students do not completely understand how to identify which sources they've used on
a research project, for example. Some educators do
not like to use the word *plagiarism* to describe an
unintentional act. They prefer to call that a "misuse
of sources."[4]

In order to deal with the problems that come
in trying to define plagiarism, one school offers its
students a very long and detailed explanation of the
term. According to one university in New Zealand,

> *Plagiarism is presenting someone else's work as if
> it were your own, whether you mean to or not.
> 'Someone else's work' means anything that is not your
> own idea, even if it is presented in your own style. It
> includes material from books, journals or any other
> printed source, the work of other students or staff,
> information from the Internet, software programs
> and other electronic material, designs and ideas. . . .
> It also includes the organization or structuring of
> any such material. . . .*[5]

That last sentence may be a new concept for
many. It means that it's not fair for a student
having trouble with an outline to put their material for a research project in the same order or

otherwise use the same organization as in an article or book they've read.

Plagiarism is a problem everywhere. Well-established writers and journalists have been accused of plagiarism. So have politicians and businesspeople. This also includes musicians, artists, filmmakers, playwrights—and at least one weather forecaster.[6] Educators have run into serious trouble, too. One college president had to resign after he was found to have plagiarized a speech he gave to incoming students. Plagiarism is a pervasive problem. As a consequence, it's one that you're likely to hear about even after you leave school. Ten years from now, your supervisors at work may be warning you against plagiarizing, just as your teachers do now.

Original Work

One thing that will help you avoid plagiarism throughout your life is to understand what constitutes original work. The word *original* comes from the word *origin. Origin* means "beginning." So *original* is the word applied to the first of something. It can also be used to refer to something that is new or novel, meaning "fresh" or "unusual." Perhaps at some point you've heard someone say, "There is nothing new under the sun." That's a common expression. It's based on a Bible verse from the Book of Ecclesiastes.[7] People often bring it up when they're trying to explain what teachers consider original work. The point they're trying to make is that in reality, many ideas are used over and over. Think about how many times movies revolve around the boy-meets-girl plotline. Many, many writers, songwriters, playwrights, and others draw on similar experiences or imagine the same kinds of situations. Historians study the same events time and time again. Also, in some cases, people base a work on another they've seen, read, or heard. The playwright William Shakespeare based many of his plays on older Italian plays.[8]

What can be difficult for a student to understand is why it's not considered plagiarism when an author, screenwriter, or playwright uses a familiar story line. That's because they add something new. That is what students are supposed to do. Students are expected to write papers in their own words, using the words of others only when they say they're doing so. (How, exactly, they say they're doing so will be covered in chapters 4 and 5).

What Do Teachers in the United States Want Their Students to Do on a Research Project?

1. When assigned a research project, you may be given a topic. Sometimes you are allowed to choose a topic. You need to decide what interests you about the topic. That might include

your opinion on it. You are then supposed to find out what other people have already written or said about your topic.

2. Once you're done doing research, you need to put together a presentation that's new and original.[9] You should come up with your own thoughts and ideas about the topic using credible, or reliable, research as your source material. You might compare the findings of different studies, for example, or write about an experience of your own. Always make sure to credit your source material.

3. As much as possible, you should use your own words and your own voice to explain what you have found out.

Why Do People Plagiarize?

Teachers expect students to turn in original work that includes their own ideas. They want to see a computer program, for example, that a student has written alone or as part of a group project. They wish to read a short story that comes from a student's imagination, rather than one based on a movie he or she saw last summer. And they want to see evidence in a research paper on the civil rights movement that the student has come to understand how much courage it took for Rosa Parks to refuse to move from her seat on the bus.

Yet teachers today often see work that is not original. In some extreme cases, an entire project has been copied. Other times, sections of a paper aren't the student's original work. And some students take a little bit from another source for their projects, without giving credit. In all three cases, it's plagiarism.

Why do students plagiarize? In surveys and interviews, students give different answers. Some students believe cheating is widespread throughout American culture. Sad to say, they believe it is acceptable. A few students simply regard school as not worth a great deal of effort. They don't see why it's important to do good work. Some do not believe that a teacher could be interested in what they have to say. A large percentage of students who admit to plagiarizing say they do it because they run out of time, not allotting enough time to complete an assignment. Some say they have to do it because they're under tremendous pressure to succeed. Students sometimes pressure themselves to get excellent grades. Other times, the pressure comes from a parent.[10] Some parents put a lot of pressure on their children about their grades. They might do so because they feel it's important for their children to get into a certain college or graduate school or land a great job after graduation.

More often, students plagiarize because they don't know what the rules are. In fact, when teachers accuse students of plagiarism, the students are often very surprised. They plead ignorance. And many instructors believe this is true, that the students do not understand what they've done wrong. Educators say schools are not doing enough to teach students how to avoid plagiarizing. Classes

From the Teacher's Point of View

Teachers who are worried about plagiarism often talk about the problem among themselves. They compare notes. They exchange stories about what they've seen. The types of plagiarism that many teachers have seen include:

- a "recycled" paper, which a student has already turned in for another class;

- a beautifully worded paper turned in by a student who has had trouble writing all his previous assignments;

- two papers, exactly the same, turned in by two different people taking the same class;

- a paper about which a student, when asked, could answer no questions;

- a paper that was purchased, probably off the Internet (in one case, a professor says he got a paper from a boy who didn't realize that it had been written by a girl and thus had personal stories that clearly weren't his).[11]

don't spend enough time explaining how to take good notes and then use them to write a research project.[12] It's left up to students to learn why plagiarism—and illegal downloading—are important and what must be done to avoid them.

Academic Cheating

Educators say they see more plagiarism lately. In fact, they say they witness more and more cheating in general. And the statistics support these statements. One study conducted in 1969 found that around half of all students let other students copy their work. Today, the rate is 97.5 percent.[13] On most campuses, 70 percent of students admit to doing some kind of cheating.[14] Their offenses vary widely, but they're all wrong.

The many forms of academic cheating include:

- cheating on tests (whether copying off another student's paper; using a cell phone to text message someone, asking for an answer; or using a cheat sheet of some type);

- plagiarizing;

- falsifying data for a lab report;

- making up sources for a research project;

- cooperating with other students on projects when the instructor has said this is not allowed.

Chapter 2

Types of Plagiarism

IN SOME CASES, students who plagiarize know exactly what they're doing. They set out to deceive their teachers, to fool them into thinking that they're turning in original work. These students want to receive good grades but are unwilling to earn them by doing the work required. And so they somehow come up with papers that are not theirs and turn them in. In other cases, students plagiarize in just a small section of a project, often without knowing they're doing so.

Some school honor codes call for people who are caught to be punished based on the amount of material plagiarized or the type of plagiarism involved. In other cases, honor codes have one punishment for all forms of plagiarism—whether it is an entire paper or a single sentence.

Buying (or Borrowing) a Paper

Let's say students receive an assignment to write a paper or do a lab. Maybe they're feeling lazy and don't want to do the work. Or they might not like a

Both high schools and colleges often have honor codes that spell out what conduct they expect from their students. These codes often specifically talk about plagiarism and its consequences.

For example, W. T. Woodson High School of Fairfax, Virginia, defines the word *plagiarize* to mean "steal and pass off . . . as one's own . . . without crediting the source." It says that plagiarizing is not limited to words, specifically mentioning "structure, ideas, pattern of thought, sequence of ideas, programming or computer code" as well. It says all students must do their work without plagiarizing and warns them that teachers are required to check papers for plagiarism and to give a zero or F to work that is found to be plagiarized.[1]

The Illinois Mathematics and Science Academy says that to plagiarize is "to make it appear in [one's] writing as if [another's] writing, including text, stories or narratives, thoughts, or discovered facts are [one's] own, or to represent the artistic creation or graphic or tabular presentation [graphs and charts, for example] of others as [one's] own." It leaves it up to a teacher to deal with what it calls a breach of academic integrity, but warns students that punishments range "from warnings and conferences . . . to probation, suspension and dismissal, or any combination thereof."[2]

A Connecticut private school named Choate Rosemary Hall requires students to write this honor pledge on every single paper they turn in: "On my honor, I have neither given nor received unauthorized aid on this assignment."[3]

class or an instructor. But perhaps they're carrying a heavy course load and feel they don't have enough time to get all their assignments done. Whatever the reason, students sometimes hand in an assignment for which they have done no work.[4]

They may have gotten a paper from the Web. There are sites that let people download papers for free. These sites offer all kinds of materials—from American history reports to book reports—already written by other people. There are many more Web sites that sell research papers. "Paper mills"—as companies that sell reports, essays, and papers to students are often called—advertise in university newspapers. Students sometimes find them by using "papers for sale" in an Internet search. In some cases, students find out about paper mills through word of mouth. One student simply tells another about a paper mill he's heard about or used.

Students who use paper mills don't know that instructors now have access to many tools that help them uncover plagiarism. There are plenty of anti-plagiarism services available that permit teachers to easily check to see if a student's paper is readily available out there in cyberspace.[5] Many schools also now give teachers extensive training on how to detect plagiarism on their own. As a result, teachers are becoming better and better at identifying instances of plagiarism. And it is now easier to prove that a plagiarized work is not a student's real writing.

Using the Web to Catch Plagiarism

As more and more educators begin to realize that plagiarism is a very serious problem among American students, they look for new and better ways to detect it. One way is to use Web sites that check papers electronically. Examples include Turnitin and iThenticate. Teachers simply submit part or all of a student's paper. Turnitin checks against billions of pages of material in books, magazines, and other sources to see if even a few words have been copied.[6] As the checking systems become more advanced, it will be even easier and faster for teachers to catch plagiarists. Now that's something to think about when using sources without credit!

In other situations, students have gotten their hands on a ready-made paper through some other means. Students sometimes hire someone else to do their paper, or they buy papers from other students. Other times an upperclassman will sell his freshman English essay. Students also "borrow" other people's papers. They might ask to use a paper written by an older sister or a friend. Some students even stoop to stealing papers. They figure out where another student or a professor keeps old papers and go into a file drawer or onto a computer without permission. Sometimes they go to the trouble of retyping the paper they steal. Other times students simply photocopy an old paper, adding a new title page. They don't realize how serious the consequences will be if they're caught doing so—or how likely it is they will be caught.

Students also sometimes "recycle" their own papers, turning in a paper for one class that they wrote for another. This act is referred to as self-plagiarism.[7] No one—neither students nor professional writers—should self-plagiarize. In a book called *Plagiarism and Originality*, Alexander Lindley explains why it's wrong for professional writers to do this. For example, let's say an author has published a book with one publisher. Now he doctors it a little and talks a new publisher into publishing the slightly altered book. Lindley says, "If [an author] takes a published work of his, alters it here and there, and puts it forward under a new title, he wrongs his first publisher, cheats the second, and swindles his readers. And if the original copyright is held by someone else, both he and his second publisher become liable for infringement."[8] (The original copyright may still be held by someone else if, for example, the first publisher still holds the copyright for the original published version. In this case, the author is not just plagiarizing himself, he is also stealing from the the first publisher.)

Copying for a Project

Sometimes students may put together a paper themselves, but they copy some of the material they put in it. Occasionally, they will copy from just one source. It's much more common, however, for students to take material from more than one source. Sometimes they put in large sections of text they did not write. Other times, they include just a sentence or two here and there. Or they may pick up just one key phrase from another author. It does not matter. Teachers see all of these cases as plagiarism.

Often, students copy material from the Internet. Some students are confused and think that anything online is available for the taking. This is absolutely not true. Copying from the Internet is no different than copying from anywhere else. Students also copy material from printed sources. They "lift" sections of a book or a magazine article. This is wrong. It doesn't

Busted!

Teachers have lots of tricks up their sleeves that they use when they're considering whether they are looking at a plagiarized paper. Here are some questions they ask themselves: Does the student seem to have paid attention to what was asked for? In other words, was this paper written for *this* assignment? Is the writing in the paper perfect? (That's a great warning sign—few students can produce that.) Does the paper sound like the student I know? (Of course, many students try to write better than they speak. Teachers do realize this.) Are her sources up-to-date? Would they be available in the school or local library?[9] In the long run, teachers weigh many factors in an effort to decide whether students are capable of writing papers they turn in.

matter if the student is copying from last week's *Newsweek* or a book that was published one hundred years ago. Older material may be in the public domain, or no longer under copyright. Nevertheless, to copy without saying one is doing so is to plagiarize. And another thing students must not do is to translate material from a foreign language book and turn it in as their own work.

The Misuse of Sources

Experts say that too many students come out of high school not having learned enough about plagiarism. They do not know all the ins and outs of how to write a paper. They make mistakes in how they use sources. They do not know how or when to give credit.

When to Credit Other People's Work

- When you quote them directly, using their exact words
- When you use the gist, or the general idea, of what they're saying
- When you state their opinion
- When you use statistics you have not gathered
- When you insert a chart or graph you yourself did not make
- When you insert an image that wasn't made by you[10]

Students sometimes include a direct quotation in a paper or a multimedia presentation without using quotation marks. Sometimes students will include a quote, but do not say whom they are quoting.

At other times, students paraphrase someone else's words. Paraphrasing is reproducing "the exact sense of a written passage or oral statement in your own words."[11] *Sense* is the key word there. Students are not allowed to rewrite or reword sentences or paragraphs from a book or article unless they indicate they're doing so.

It's considered plagiarism when a writer follows another person's work too closely. Of course it's unfair to use another person's words. But students are also not supposed to follow the other person's sentence or paragraph structure, either. They cannot put their ideas together in exactly the same way as someone else. And it's generally considered plagiarism when a writer uses someone else's ideas without acknowledgment.

In some cases, this may seem obvious. Imagine you're writing a paper about the assassination of President John F. Kennedy. Even though it happened more than forty years ago, it's still a very controversial subject. People have a wide variety of opinions concerning how and why he was killed. It would be a student's responsibility in his paper to say whose opinion he's putting forth. Gerald Posner wrote in his book *Case Closed* that he believes the assassin Lee Harvey Oswald acted alone. But in his book *Ultimate Sacrifice,* Lamar Waldron says he thinks the Central Intelligence Agency—the branch of the federal government that helps with national security by collecting information about other countries and groups—at least knew about the plot in advance. If students read these books and wanted to include their ideas, then they must make it clear that they are doing so. The name of the author and the title of the book should be explicitly mentioned in the paper, in addition to being included in the bibliography and any footnotes or endnotes.

There are other cases, however, in which a student doesn't draw on huge ideas, but merely takes facts from a variety of sources. In writing a biographical essay about President George W. Bush, for example, a student might look at several different biographies. Some may offer a lot of information about his childhood, while others may talk at length about the years that he was in the oil business. In this case, it's considered plagiarism if the student does not indicate the sources in which specific facts or statistics were found.

One complicating factor is that teachers do not require students to cite their source for what's called common knowledge. Dr. Miguel Roig says in one manual on avoiding plagiarism that writers don't have to provide a citation in cases where "everybody knows that."[12] What does this mean? When writing papers, students should assume that only very basic facts are common knowledge—for example, that there are fifty states, or that Martin Luther King, Jr., was a civil rights leader.

Common Knowledge

Although students are told to cite sources for the information they use in a research paper, there is one exception to this rule—common knowledge. This includes very familiar facts, such as the fact that George Washington was the first president of the United States or that Los Angeles is in the state of California. There's no need to create a note for information like this.

Plagiarism in Creative Writing

Most of the time, schools and instructors seem most concerned about plagiarism in research projects. However, students need to avoid plagiarism when working on all kinds of school projects. It's important not to plagiarize when writing a research paper or putting together an oral or multimedia presentation. Students have also been charged with plagiarism on lab reports, computer programs, and technical studies. And although it might not seem possible at first, some people commit plagiarism when doing creative writing.

When students are in a class—whether it's English or creative writing or history—it's against the rules for them to put their name on a poem or short story that they did not write.[13] It may be permissible to include in a poem a line from another poem as an homage, so to speak. (To make an homage is to indicate respect for something.) For example, a poet might include a line or a phrase by the poet T. S. Eliot that he finds absolutely crucial to his own work, as a tribute to Eliot and to enrich the meaning of his own poem. The poet usually wants the reader to recognize the line and consider it while reading his poem. (In fact, Eliot himself liked to include bits of others' works in his poems.) But it's essential for a student to let their teacher know they've done this. They could do this in a conversation when they turn in the paper or attach a note to their work. They could also use quotation marks or italics to set apart the words that aren't

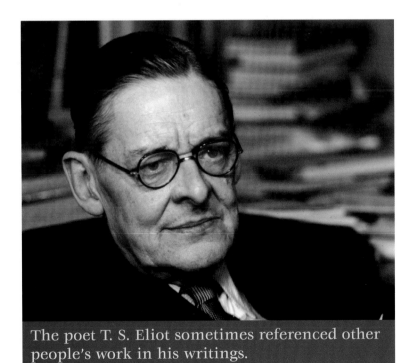

The poet T. S. Eliot sometimes referenced other people's work in his writings.

theirs, and make a notation about it at the bottom of the page.

In some cases, writers of literary works, such as novels, short stories, or comic books, are inspired by someone else's plot or characters. In fact, there's a modern phenomenon called fanfiction, or fanfic for short. Fans write all kinds of fiction based on movies, TV shows, and graphic novels.[14] They post a lot of it on Web sites. This is acceptable when it is only for their own enjoyment or to amuse their friends. But if they somehow make money doing so—if they sell what they write—they are guilty of copyright infringement.[15]

The opportunities to write fanfiction and get school credit for it are probably very limited. Still, there is a problem in schools when students turn in creative work that they've based on something they've seen or read. To avoid any problems, it's a good idea for a student to talk to a teacher before getting started on a story that's been inspired by another work. Even if the teacher agrees to the project, the student might want to attach something to the final version of the story to explain and identify the source of the inspiration. This will serve as a reminder to the teacher and ensure there are no questions about the nature of the project.

Outside of School

Again, students aren't the only ones held accountable for plagiarizing. It occurs at work as well, and not just with professional writers. Filmmakers have also been accused. In 1997, an author named Barbara Chase-Riboud sued Steven Spielberg and his film and television production company, DreamWorks. She claimed that their movie, *Amistad,* had used characters from a novel she had written about the same slave rebellion. She later dropped the lawsuit. Some people speculated she and DreamWorks had settled the lawsuit out of court, although that is not known for certain.

Politicians also have come under fire. In 1987, Senator Joe Biden wanted to run for president but had to drop out of the race after it was proved he had plagiarized one of his speeches.

Most frequently, however, it's authors and journalists who are accused. In 2002, a famous historian named Stephen Ambrose was accused by a journalist of plagiarizing in no less than six of his best-selling titles. There was no copyright infringement lawsuit filed. But Ambrose had to admit to the public what he'd done, which must have been embarrassing for him. Within just a few short weeks, another famous historian, Doris Kearns Goodwin, admitted that a book she published in 1987 called *The Fitzgeralds and the Kennedys* included many passages taken from other sources. In her case, she asked her publisher to destroy unsold copies of her book, which she planned to rewrite. She also took a leave of absence from a television job in order to be able to concentrate on the problem.[16]

A journalist named Jayson Blair had to resign from his job at *The New York Times* after it was found out that he plagiarized in some of his stories, and also made up facts. The situation came to light when an editor noticed that an article about a Texas military family that appeared under Blair's byline in *The New York Times* was almost identical to one that appeared in a San Antonio paper. The article seemed to indicate the author had spent time with the family. Blair couldn't even prove that he had been to Texas. He resigned because of this in May 2003.[17]

In 2005, a reporter from India was asked to stop writing for American newspapers after it was discovered he was including words from a British newspaper in his articles. A local newspaper in Worcester, Massachusetts, made one of its sports reporters come home early from covering the Super Bowl after the editor discovered that he had plagiarized something from *Sports Illustrated* magazine in an article he wrote about the event.[18] The next year it was discovered that a columnist named Ben Domenech, who wrote a blog for *The Washington Post* newspaper, had been plagiarizing for years. He started plagiarizing when he was in college. He had to apologize and resign, which was embarrassing and might also hurt his future career. Also in 2006 were the well-known cases of Kaavya Viswanathan and Dan Brown, the author of the very famous *The Da Vinci Code*. He felt very relieved after a court decided he did not, in fact, plagiarize in his best-selling book.

Chapter 3

Understanding Copyright and Fair Use

PLAGIARISM IS CONSIDERED A VERY SERIOUS form of academic cheating. Relatively few students go so far as to buy a paper rather than write one of their own. There are plenty of individuals, however, who do a cut-and-paste job when they're assigned a research project. They create an outline and then go through books and Web sites, looking for text they can insert in the appropriate places. Others stick in just a sentence or two here or there that they didn't write themselves.

For a long time, cheating on assignments was the focus of school administrators' concern. Lately, however, more and more schools have also developed policies that prohibit students from performing illegal downloads. They don't want young people to use school computers in a way that infringes on copyright law. They're trying to keep both schools and students out of trouble.

Learning more about copyrights and the fair use guidelines is one of the best ways to prevent copyright infringement and plagiarism. Once the rules are clear, it will be easier to use different types of media both inside and outside school.

Copyright 101

When the U.S. Constitution was written in 1787, the creators of this important document gave Congress the "power . . . to promote the progress of science and useful arts, by securing for limited times to authors and inventors the exclusive right to their respective writings and discoveries."[1] This meant they were given the right to benefit from their creations and inventions—to be given credit for them and to make money from them. In 1797, the first Congress enacted the Copyright Act, which served to protect the rights of authors to say how and when their books would be published.

Since then, the Copyright Act has been revised many times, four times in very significant ways. Mostly, the act has been expanded to include other sorts of works besides books. The last major revision occurred in 1976, but the law has been added to many times since then. This has been necessary, especially because of the development of the Internet, as well as the invention of many technological devices, including the personal computer, the CD player, the MP3 player, and the DVD player. The copyright law is now contained in a massive document that has become so big, it's divided into thirteen chapters. At its end are nine appendices, or additions.[2]

Understanding Copyright and Fair Use

Today, copyrights protect literary works (including books, magazine and newspaper articles, scripts, poems, and blogs), visual arts (including paintings, photographs, and sculptures), performing arts (including plays, movies, and choreographs or dance-step sequences), sound recordings, computer software, and more. Copyright is automatically established when a work is recorded—when its words or musical notes are written down or a scene is captured on film. The establishment of a copyright gives creators the right to decide when their works can be used and/or reproduced throughout their entire lives. This can be very important for authors, for example, who earn their living by writing.

But copyright also matters for other, less tangible reasons. People's creations are very important to them. A photographer who has taken a photograph of a beautiful place in the remote wilds may not want it to be used to illustrate an article encouraging tourists to travel there. A composer may not want his music to be used in a movie he doesn't like. For works created in the United States after 1978, the creator's heirs retain copyright protection for another seventy years after the creator's death. For works created before 1978, the law is more complicated. The period of time in which rights are protected after a creator's death varies, according to when the work was published. But after a copyright runs out, or expires, works enter the public domain.

What is the public domain? This can be hard to understand. The word *domain* is often used to refer to a place, a territory, or an area that's ruled or controlled by a person or group or government. Put *public* and *domain* together, and the resulting term has two meanings. It can mean land that is owned by a government. But it also applies to creative works that are owned or controlled by the people. Works in the public domain can be used by anyone. Some of these works have never been copyrighted. That was especially true in the old days, when an author or a company had to file

Works in the public domain can be used by anyone.

paperwork in order to establish a copyright. Some people did not know how to do this, while others simply did not want to bother.

Government agencies often create works that are intended for people to copy. An agency may want to get information out to as many people as possible—especially if it has to do with health or safety. But how do people find out which works are in the public domain? Readers can check a book, for example, to see if it has a copyright notice on the back of its title page or elsewhere in the book. And librarians can help students and other patrons find out whether something's in the public domain. They may well warn them, however, that just because a work is in the public domain doesn't mean students can copy it without saying they're doing so.

The law currently says copyright is automatically established when a work is created. Sometimes creators are content with the copyright that is automatically established. Often, however, they take an additional step. They register their copyright. The U.S. Copyright Office says that this is how a public record of the copyright is made. It also points out that the law says registration is necessary if a creator wants to be able to file an infringement lawsuit. When someone files a lawsuit, or sues, the lawsuit goes to court to be decided by a judge. In the past, it was not necessary to register a copyright in order to sue for copyright infringement. Today it is.

Courts hear copyright lawsuits on a regular basis. Authors or publishers might sue if their books are reprinted without their permission. Writers may think about suing when they believe a filmmaker is ripping off an idea that was theirs, making a movie based on a book they've written. A songwriter might take a film company to court if his or her song is used in a movie without permission. Record producers, filmmakers, and software companies sue over bootlegs—unauthorized CDs, DVDs, and computer programs.

Plagiarism—using another person's work without giving credit—is unfair. It's wrong. A student—or anyone else—who does it gets in trouble. Committing plagiarism has ruined people's lives. Yet even though it's so serious, there's no law against that precise act.

Sometimes plagiarism is also copyright infringement, such as when an author copies someone else's copyrighted work, without credit or appropriate permission, to be published and sold in their own book. Copyright infringement is against the law.

When someone downloads a copyrighted song without paying for it, that's copyright infringement. When a person uses an Internet site that allows file sharing to download a copy of a new video game from another user without paying for it, that's copyright infringement. When a person goes online to download a commercial she saw during this year's Super Bowl, and puts it up on her Web site, that's copyright infringement. In all these cases, the person is breaking the law.

There are other forms of copying besides downloading that are also illegal. When someone copies a friend's software, putting it on their own computer, that's copyright infringement. If a person copies a scene from a recently released DVD and puts it up on their Web site, that's copyright infringement. And if a reader photocopies a friend's new graphic novel, that's copyright infringement, too.

Sometimes courts decide in favor of the copyright holder. But other times, they decide that the copyright was not infringed on. That's often because of something called the fair use doctrine.

What Is Fair Use?

It's acceptable for students to quote—to use word for word—the work of others in reports and other school projects if they credit the source in their text, notes, and/or a bibliography. There are special rules to be learned that must be followed when they want to quote directly from a book, magazine, Web site, or other source. At school, these rules are often laid out in honor codes. Teachers often go over them when assigning research papers. Very simple rules state that students should not copy when writing papers. Sometimes school or teacher rules are more specific—they might talk about how many quotes a paper can include, for example, or how long quotes should be. For instance, there might be restrictions on how much material can be quoted from another source or instructions on exactly how to show where the quote came from.

What can be very confusing for students is the fact that there are special rules that apply when materials are used outside of school assignments— for a magazine article or on a Web site, for example. U.S. copyright law, which protects the rights of creators to decide how their work will be used, has a special section that covers what is called fair use. According to the law, there are some limits as to creators' control. The law says it is fair for writers, musicians, educators, and other people to use copyrighted material without permission in certain cases. These are when the material is being used for the purposes of criticism, comment, or instruction.

Neither adults nor students are likely to understand what "criticism, comment, or instruction" means at first glance. Let's consider these terms one by one. Criticism, in this case, refers to what are called reviews. A review is a piece published in a newspaper, magazine, or on the Web. It can be about a book, a CD, a concert, a movie, a show at an art gallery, or a theater production, among other things. In it, the author—called the reviewer—states his opinion of the book or other media. He says whether he liked it or not. He often goes into specifics as to what he liked or did not like. Readers read reviews and decide whether to go out and buy a book or see a movie. The fair use clause in U.S. copyright law means a reviewer can quote, or repeat words from, a book. Likewise, he can quote the lyrics from a music CD in a review of that CD (even if he doesn't like it).

Second, there's comment. The law also says writers are allowed to comment on others' work. So if a person writing a newspaper editorial— which states an opinion—wants to discuss what a politician said in a speech, he or she can repeat what the senator said, word for word. Another example would be a historian who can use quotes from another historian to illustrate a point in her own work. She should say where exactly the quote came from, but she doesn't need to get permission to use it.

Parody and Fair Use

One thing it might surprise you to learn is that the fair use clause allows writers to parody (or make fun of) something. That's why *Mad* magazine, for example, can "send up" blockbuster movies and TV shows. The late-night talk-show host Jay Leno is allowed to quote from movies he finds funny. What is not considered fair use, however, is repackaging someone's work or competing with it. The bottom line is that only the creator is supposed to profit from their own work. The copyright attorney Lloyd Jassin sums up fair use in this statement:

> Fair use is a privilege. It permits authors, scholars, researchers and educators to borrow small portions of a copyrighted work for socially productive purposes without asking permission or paying a fee.[3]

It's important to note that he says "small portions." There is no set limit—like twenty lines of poetry or 250 words or twelve bars of a song—that can be used. Courts say that what's important is that the substance of a work is not copied.[4]

It's also considered fair use to make fun of something. That's sometimes called doing a parody. It's considered another form of comment. Finally, there's the matter of instruction, which is a fancy word for teaching. Teachers are allowed to use

Journalists listen to a speech by Hillary Clinton.

copyrighted materials when they're teaching students. And journalists are allowed to summarize speeches and use facts gathered by other people, for example, in news reports.[5] That's also considered instruction or education, even though it's outside of the classroom.

Sometimes there are lawsuits filed in which a person is accused of copyright infringement. Judges and juries then determine whether there is a fair use involved. They ask four questions:

1. What is the purpose and character of the use? In other words, why did the person who used the material want to use it: Was it for criticism, comment, or instruction?
2. What is the nature—the type—of the work used?
3. How much of the work is used?
4. What effect would the use have on the market for the original?[6] This question has to do with whether the new work will mean that the creator of the original will now have trouble selling his own work.

There are no official guidelines for how much of a work can be referenced under the terms of fair use. It is important, however, to look at the relationship between the quoted material and the whole work. You always want to make sure you are only using a small section, never a substantial portion of the material. And remember, no matter what, to indicate where you obtained your information or quote. Taking good notes during the research phase of a project is a good way to avoid confusion over the source of any of your information.

The Fair Use of Material on Web Sites

Sometimes students create a Web site for a class. Other times, they do so for a club or their own enjoyment. It's not acceptable for people to post material on their sites that they have not created unless they have asked to do so. Web designers are not supposed to exactly copy other people's Web sites in terms of how they look or are organized. You can look at sites for ideas as to what you might like to do, but it's important, as always, that your work be your own. And of course, you cannot download content from another person's Web page and put it up on yours. It doesn't matter whether you'd like to use someone else's words, artwork, photographs, music, or video clip. To do this, you must have permission. You also can't scan a copyrighted work—whether it's part of a book or a piece of artwork or a photo—and put it up.[7] You can't put up even a little bit of the latest song that you like.

Many companies prevent other people from using their Web page content by using special programs called spiders. Spiders can search for exact matches in images and text. The Fox Network is one company that actively searches for personal Web sites that use its images and music. When it finds an individual who's doing so, the network first sends what is called a cease-and-desist letter to request that the person stop using its materials. Later on, the company might take legal action.[8]

What about when you're writing material for a blog or your Web site? Perhaps you want to create something based on someone's work. Remember that the fair use doctrine says you're allowed to parody a copyrighted work but that you can't use it in other ways (writing a sequel to your favorite murder mystery and trying to sell it, for example). Also keep in mind that you're allowed to quote short sections from a work—it doesn't matter whether it's a book, a movie, or a music CD—if you're posting a review. You can give the titles of books, CDs, and other materials. But you can't include copyrighted text on your blog or Web site unless you're doing a review or a send-up. Using dialogue from a hit movie could get you a cease-and-desist letter.[9]

Finally, what do you need to know about creating links? If you just use words or a URL to lead your user to another Web page, that's fine. But you cannot use a copyrighted image to link to another site unless you have permission. So don't use the Nike swoosh to link to that company's Web page!

Chapter 4

Finding Sources and Taking Good Notes

MANY STUDENTS DREAD being assigned a research project. One common reason is because they're not very comfortable with the process. Perhaps they do not feel confident that they know what to do. When this is the case, one thing that will help is to go to the library or bookstore. There are many books out there that deal specifically with how to do research or write a research paper. For help in finding one, ask a librarian. Librarians will also be able to direct students to some style guides. A style guide offers rules for writing, including instructions on how to punctuate, capitalize, and create footnotes or endnotes and a bibliography. One guide that many high school teachers like is by William B. Strunk, Jr. and E. B. White.[1] It's titled *The Elements of Style.* Teachers also often recommend students look for the *MLA Handbook* or *The Chicago Manual of Style.*[2] In

A good research project usually begins with a trip to the library.

college classes, professors sometimes ask students to use a special style, like that adopted by the American Psychological Association (APA). They will refer you to the right style guide to use.

What Is the Purpose of a Research Project?

Perhaps you wonder why instructors assign research projects. They like research projects because they offer their students a different way—other than sitting and listening to a lecture or reading in a textbook—to learn about the subject of their class. Research projects help students learn how to gather information. They can also teach students how to use information, to generate their own ideas, and to support them. Students also need to learn how to choose sources and cite them. To cite sources is to acknowledge use of them.

There are two types of research papers. The first is the analytical paper (in high school, these are sometimes called term papers). In papers like this, students present and analyze information they've found on a topic. The second type of paper is argumentative. Sometimes that's called a thesis paper. In the argumentative paper, a student "uses evidence to attempt to convince the reader of [his or her] particular stance on a debatable topic."[3] In both cases, students will mostly be putting together facts first gleaned by other people. This does not mean, however, that they'll be copying others.

Consider what Melissa Walker, the author of a book about writing research papers, wrote: "Though most of the time you will be researching what is known, your research report will still be original: You will be the one to make sense of the facts and to arrive at your own conclusions."[4] What does she mean by conclusions? Those are the positions you reach after considering facts and making connections between them. Both types of papers will require you to explain clearly what you have found, integrating, or weaving together, what you've learned from different sources. Research projects force you to put ideas in order. And because teachers almost always ask you to turn in endnotes or footnotes and a bibliography with them, they teach you how to document, or cite, your sources, too.[5]

Before You Start Your Research Project

Perhaps your teacher has talked to your class about avoiding plagiarism while writing a research paper. Or maybe you've read your school's honor code and are scared by what you've read about the penalties it imposes on plagiarists. Avoiding plagiarism may worry some students. Others will find it more of a pain. Fortunately, there are specific steps you can take to avoid committing plagiarism.

As a first step, you must actively decide to create independent work. That means you must be willing to spend time thinking about your topic. Realize that you're going to have to reach the point where you can explain in your own words what you've learned. You're also going to have to apply your critical thinking skills. That means analyzing information, considering the meaning of the facts you've gathered.

As a second step, you also have to commit to taking writing seriously. You are going to have to choose words carefully and decide how to put them together. You'll need to find your own words to express what you've learned and figured out. How can you do this? Imagine you're explaining your topic to a classmate. Make an effort to avoid words that strike you as boring or vague. It may help you stay clear if you stick to short sentences. When you're writing, periodically try out your words, reading them out loud. See where you stumble. That might be a place where you need to restructure your sentence or think of better words to use. What if you can't come up with other words on your own? Consult a dictionary or thesaurus.

How to Avoid Plagiarism in Research Projects

- Make sure you allot enough time to your project. Keep your deadline in mind so that you're not in a rush to write or finish up your project.

- Select your topic carefully. Choose something that interests you. If you are excited about your topic, you will want to do well on your project. If you need help coming up with a research topic, feel free to ask your teacher for help. Librarians might have ideas, too.

- Use a wide variety of sources.

- Take good notes, keeping careful track of what's a quotation and what's a paraphrase or summary.

- Keep track of your sources.

- When you're putting together your final project, integrate the facts you've gathered. Weave them together in your own way.

- Cite your sources.

- Double-check all quotations, making sure that you are using exactly the same words and punctuation that appeared in the source.[6]

Another way to avoid plagiarism is to pay attention when your teacher makes an assignment. The number one thing to find out is the deadline. One of the major reasons people commit plagiarism is starting a paper or project too late.[7] They get rushed. This is particularly dangerous if they do not have enough time to take notes, but have to research and write at the same time. One way to avoid getting in trouble is to set yourself specific goals while looking at your calendar. Pencil in when you want to be ready to move from one stage to the next. This will help you to make steady progress, moving from working on your concept to creating an outline to undertaking the research to writing your paper. Make sure to leave enough time to do the final wrap-up stuff that a paper requires, like creating a title page and a bibliography.

So you've double-checked and know exactly when your assignment is due. You've given some thought to how you're going to use your time. Next, you need to think about the project and decide what you're going to do. When teachers give an assignment, it's important to pay close attention to what they want. They might be expecting a term paper, which summarizes research. On the other hand, they might want a thesis paper, which presents and supports an argument. Whichever is the case, if they talk about the project in class, take notes. If they pass out or post on the class Web site a description of the assignment, read it over carefully. Go back and look at it a couple of times during the project to make sure you're still on track. If you have trouble understanding what they want, ask. Don't be afraid. If you feel too embarrassed to speak up in front of other students or if there isn't enough time during class, speak to your instructors outside of class.

Ready to Research

Even in cases where instructors tell you what your research project is going to cover, you often have to decide exactly how you're going to focus your paper. Let's say you've been given a specific research assignment: You are supposed to find out what role Americans played in World War II. This is an enormous topic. You will not be able to cover all of it in any research project. You're going to have to narrow down the topic. How do you do this? Sometimes you will be assigned a research project on a topic you already know a great deal about. More often, you won't know very much at all. Whatever the case, one good way to start is by asking yourself what, specifically, you'd like to find out about your topic.

In this particular case, you might ask yourself how the U.S. military became involved in the war. Maybe you'd like to know specifically how African Americans contributed to the war effort. Maybe you're interested in whether there were German, Italian, or Japanese Americans who went to fight in their homelands. It's a good idea to try to come up with two or three ideas, so that you'll have a choice, should you not be able to find enough information about one of the topics. When considering ideas, bear in mind advice offered by Jeffrey Strausser, the author of *Painless Writing*. He says, "Your topic should challenge you, rather than overwhelm or confuse you. . . . You won't impress

Sometimes you'll go to a library to look up a subject but won't find what you're looking for, or perhaps you can't find enough sources. In either case, you're going to have to use your detective skills. Think first about the terms you used to search the library catalog. A librarian might help you if you can't come up with new ones.

One good way to start a research project is by using what are called reference tools. That's what librarians call sources that you refer to, rather than read. Reference tools include works like dictionaries, encyclopedias, yearbooks, atlases, gazetteers, statistical sources, and biographical dictionaries.[8] At large libraries, you'll also find specialized reference books, like encyclopedias of botany. Libraries might also have government documents and local history materials in their reference collections. Some reference tools come in electronic formats, such as online or CD-ROM databases.

One thing you can do once you have located one good source is to check to see what sources its author relied on. Look at his or her footnotes or endnotes and bibliography. Note other sources that seem to you like they might be useful, and look for them. You can also look to see what subject headings have been assigned to a book. To do that, go back to the library catalog and look up the book you're looking at. The subject headings that were assigned to it will appear at the bottom of the book's catalog entry. Use those subject headings to search for other relevant sources in the library catalog. If you like to research on the Internet, do a Web search using the topic of your paper as a search term.

your teacher by turning in page after page of information that he or she knows you do not understand. . . . Similarly, do not choose a topic that is below your understanding level because the object of the term paper is to provide you with an opportunity to learn more about a topic that interests you."[9]

If you can't come up with a focus for your project, you can also talk to your teacher. It also might be a good idea to look for some general books about World War II or U.S. history between 1939 and 1945. If you have an idea of the questions you're going to try to answer in your project, you might also look for books that are more specific. You could look for books about African Americans in the military, for example.

In any case, unless you know your specific angle, you might want to pull several books off the library shelf. Scan their tables of contents and indexes. Start to read here and there within the books. Think about ways you could narrow your topic. At the same time, you need to make sure your topic is big enough, so that you'll be able to write the required number of pages. Set aside in a special pile the books you really like or find useful. What if you're not ready to check them out of the library? Before you go home, make a list of what they are, noting their authors, titles, and call numbers. Do not worry about getting complete bibliographic information at this point. Wait to do that until you've focused your paper and are ready to begin the research phase. If you're going to use more than one library for this project, you'll also need to note which library you found your books in.

Doing the Real Research

Once you have a project idea, you might want to mull it over for at least a short while. Melissa Walker, the author of a guide to writing research papers, says, "Live with your ideas for a while; let them brew."[10] After all, you need to come up with a topic you're going to be happy to spend a lot of time on. If you're truly interested, you'll be less tempted to plagiarize because you'll have plenty of stuff of your own to say. When you find a topic that you think you'll enjoy, it's a good idea to talk it over with your instructor. He or she might be able to help you fine-tune your idea. Also, this will give him or her a chance to warn you if he or she thinks you're off track or if you've misunderstood the assignment.

Once you've chosen a topic and talked it over with your instructor, create an initial outline based on your preliminary research. In this you will lay out your approach to your topic. You will decide how your paper will be divided up. You might also know how you think you might subdivide your major sections. It will help very much to have a good outline before you do a lot of research. Working from an outline will help guide you as you collect information that will support what you want to say about your topic. Later on, you can develop a final outline.[11]

After you've completed your outline, go back to the sources you looked at in the beginning of your research. Once you've plumbed them for information useful to you, look for additional sources. Deliberately set out to find a variety of sources. If you're writing about the experiences of women during World War II, you might want to look for some personal journals or collected letters, for example, that have been published. Use periodical and newspaper indexes to check for relevant material in magazines and newspapers. Librarians can show you relevant full-text databases. Libraries and museums such as the Library of Congress and the Smithsonian Institution will have many Web pages devoted to life in the United States during the war or what it was like during the attack on Pearl Harbor. Remember: Do not rely entirely on any one type of source, whether it is books, magazine articles, or the Internet.

One thing you'll have to do as you go along is to evaluate, or judge the reliability of, sources. *The Little, Brown Essential Handbook for Writers* offers guidelines for evaluating print sources. It suggests you look at the publication date of the source. You want to make sure that sources you use are up-to-date. You should check to see if the book contains some information on the author, perhaps listing their credentials. You can also search the Internet for information about an author. If the author is affiliated with a university or has written other books on similar topics, you can probably consider them an expert in their field. The *Book Review Index* can lead you to reviews of the book you're using, plus others by the same author. Reviews might help you realize if an author has a particular bias. Also, the best sources clearly indicate which sources the author used. So check to see if it has footnotes, endnotes, a bibliography, or some other list of sources consulted (sometimes this is covered in an introduction).

Evaluating online sources is especially important. Remember that many Internet sources are unreliable. Individuals' Web pages are often filled with errors. Beware, too, of Wikipedia, which accepts contributions of articles from individuals, rather than soliciting them from professionals. Sometimes its articles are trustworthy, but sometimes they're not. Looking at Web sites, you should first look at their addresses (URLs), because that will tell you at least a little something about where their information comes from. Addresses end in abbreviations: edu for educational institutions, gov for government agencies, org for nonprofit organizations, mil for military organizations, and com for commercial organizations, or companies. Figuring out who sponsors a site can help you figure out its purpose.

This will let you know if a Web page about nutrition bars, say, has been put up by a certain manufacturer or a more objective source. The best sites have reliable links and list relevant sources.[12]

As you go along, it's absolutely essential that you develop what's called a working bibliography.[13] Essentially, you're going to keep a list of all the sources you use, including printed materials and material from the Web. For a very short paper, you might be able to keep a list of sources in a notebook. But for a longer paper, it's much better to do it on note cards. You might also want to use a Web tool such as NoodleBib.[14]

You must collect all the information you will need to document your paper and create a bibliography. For a book, you're going to need the author's name, the title, the city of publication, the publisher, and the date of publication. For a magazine article, you're going to need the author's name, the name of the article, the name of the periodical, the date of publication, and the page numbers of the article. It's also a good idea to write down the magazine's volume and issue number. For a Web page, write down the name of the site, the author of the page you've visited (frequently that is found at the very bottom of a Web page), the date the page was created (also found at the bottom of the page), the URL, and the date you visited the page. To find out what you're going to need for other sorts of sources, check a style guide.

A Typical Bibliography

Below are a few examples of standard formats used to cite different kinds of sources, such as newspapers, books, and Internet sites, followed by actual samples for each. These are entries you might find on a bibliography for a report on the World War II general George S. Patton. The entries follow the MLA style guidelines, which is used by many schools across the country. But always check with your teacher to see what style guide he or she wants you to use before making your bibliography.

Book

Author's Last Name, Author's First Name. <u>Title</u>. Place of publication: Publisher, date.

> Axelrod, Alan. <u>Patton: A Biography</u>. New York: Palgrave Macmillan, 2005.

Magazine Article

Author's Last Name, Author's First Name. "Title of article." <u>Title of magazine</u> dd (date as a number, if given) month (spelled out as a word) yyyy (year as four-digit number): page numbers for the article. (Note that there's no punctuation between the title of the magazine and the date. The title of the magazine and date are sometimes found at the top or bottom of a magazine page. They're always found on its cover. Some magazines do not have a date and month of publication, but just a month.)

> Kempner, M. J. "Builders at War: Seabees Beat Time and Terrain." <u>House and Garden</u> September 1945: 88–89.

Newspaper Article

Author's Last Name, Author's First Name. "Title of Newspaper Article." <u>Title of Newspaper.</u> dd (date as a number) month (spelled out as a word) yyyy (year as four-digit number): page number(s). (Note that a period separates the title of the paper from the date. The title of the paper and the date will typically be found at the top of any page of the newspaper.)

> Brett, Jennifer. "Send in the Cavalry." <u>Atlanta Journal-Constitution.</u> 30 September 2005: J9.

Scholarly Journal Article

Author's Last Name, Author's First Name. "Title of article." <u>Title of journal</u>, volume number. Issue number (year of publication): page numbers. (Scholarly journals are intended for professionals and students, rather than general readers. Please note that you only need to give the issue number if the journal numbers the pages of each issue separately. Volume and issue number can be found either on the cover or on the table of contents page.)

> Morris, Nancy J. "Beatrice Patton's Hawaii." <u>Journal of Hawaiian History</u>, 39 (2005): 75–90.

Web page

Author's Last Name, Author's First Name. "Title of Web page." <u>Title of the entire Web site</u>. Date page was posted or updated. Date when you accessed site. URL. (The author's name may appear at the beginning or end of the document. If the title does not appear at the top of a Web page, it may appear in the colored band that appears at the top of the browser window. You may need to look at the site's home page to find the site's title. The date that a page was posted or updated usually appears at the very bottom. You will need to make your own note as to when you access a site.)

> Patton, George S. "Helpful Hints to Hopeful Heroes." <u>Patton Museum of Cavalry and Armor.</u> 25 October 2001. 20 August 2006. < http://www.knox .army.mil/museum/helpful.htm > .

These are only the most basic of entries. To find out how to deal with sources that have more than one author or for which you cannot find a date of publication, for instance, consult your style guide.

How to Make Note-Taking Easier

As you find sources with useful information, you're going to need to take notes. Hey! Wait! Many readers will want to skip this section. All too often, students don't take good notes when they research. They just open up books or magazines and start copying down relevant information, word for word. When they find good information on the Web, they just use the Copy command and then Paste to transfer it to a word processing document on their computer. Be warned. Both of these practices are extremely dangerous. They are among the chief causes of plagiarism.

The best thing to do is read about a subject. This doesn't necessarily mean you have to read an

The Dangers of Copying and Pasting

When you're doing research on a Web page, copying and pasting is not recommended. Unless you take extreme care to insert quotation marks around any material you paste in *and* immediately make a footnote, including the Web page name and the URL, you are likely to lose track of which words you wrote and which you took from the author of the Web page. It's much safer to print out useful Web pages. When you do so, check the bottom of your printout to see if the URL appears there. If it does not, you will need to write it down. You should also look carefully at the Web page to see if it says when the material was posted or modified. This will let readers know when the material you're citing was created. You will also need to make a note as to when you accessed the Web page. This shows that the material was posted at that time, even if the Web page changes later.

entire source word for word—you can skim it to see if it will be useful. After you've looked through a book or read an article, decide if you're going to take notes on it. Whether you're looking at something that's been published in a book or posted on the Internet, you're going to have to make a choice. Some of what you read you can ignore. Some of it will be useful background information, but you won't necessarily need to take notes on it.

When you find material that you think you might want to use later, you need to decide whether to take notes. You've already read about how to evaluate whether a source is reliable and whether a source is relevant. Think about whether it devotes attention to your specific topic. Read a section carefully to see if it seems like the source is going to be too general or too technical. Think about how it differs from other sources you've read. Be on the lookout for sources that have a different angle or are written in an especially lively fashion, which will be good to quote from.

You also need to come up with a way to distinguish between different sorts of research notes. While doing a research project, you'll discover material you want to quote, paraphrase, interpret, or summarize. (These terms will each be each explained in detail shortly.) You could find relevant statistics or facts. And from time to time, you'll come up with a new idea or opinion on your own.[15] You must learn to take different

You have many different options when it comes to choosing a method for taking research notes. Some people do all their work on their laptop or home computer. They like to type research notes using a word-processing program such as Microsoft Word. If they're working on a small project, they might keep just one file. But larger projects will require different files, each labeled to indicate the part of the outline it pertains to. Other people like to take research notes by hand. One system that works extremely well is using note cards. Each card can be labeled at the top with a subject heading.

Whatever system you use, make sure to record the source of any information you gather as you go along. You have two choices here. You can record the complete citation every time. That means in the case of a book, write down the author, title, place of publication, publisher's name, date of publication, and relevant page numbers. In the case of a magazine, you'll need the name of the author, the title of the article, the name of the magazine, the date of publication, and the page numbers the article appears on. For a Web page, you'll need the name of the author, the title of the Web page, the title of the Web site, the date it was created or updated, and the date you accessed it.

There's also another option. You can record all this information in your working bibliography. Then in your research notes, all you'll need to record is an abbreviated reference to the individual source (you could label a note with just an author's last name or a title, plus the relevant page numbers).

kinds of research notes and how to distinguish between them.

Using Quotations Properly

What is a quotation? It's someone's exact words. You should choose what quotations you want to use very carefully. Keep in mind that the best research papers use only a few quotations. You want them to liven the paper up. Quotations also lend authority to your paper. In other words, they let the reader know what an expert—that's the authority—has said on a topic. What you do not want to do is use quotations just to fill space. Use them only when the writing is really great or you need to provide examples of other people's support for a point of view, for example.[16] Make sure quotations add something important to your paper—new information, or emphasis for a point you're trying to make.

Once you've decided to take down a quotation, you must do so extremely carefully. This is an essential step that will help you avoid plagiarism. When you're taking notes and you take down a quotation, start with a quotation mark. This is a trick you can use when taking research notes, to help you keep track of what words are not yours. One suggestion is to make it big. End with a second quotation mark. Make that one big, too. To stay absolutely on the safe side, you could write or type quotes in a special color for your notes. (Of course you will not do this when you're inserting the quotes into your actual paper!)

It's important to take careful notes during your research.

There are rules for adding words or deleting words from a quotation. If you want to start a quotation in mid-sentence, you indicate this with ellipses (. . .). You also use ellipses to indicate that you have not included the end of a sentence.

A third use for ellipses is to indicate that you have left words out in mid-sentence. If you add to a quotation or change the capitalization, punctuation, or spelling, you indicate this with brackets ([   ]). Sometimes you will see a mistake—a misspelling, for example—in the original source, but you'll still want to quote it. If you need to indicate that something in the quote is indeed as it appeared, you use [sic] right after whatever might be questionable. Write down the source, including the page number.

Here are some examples that will help you understand different ways to quote material from an original source. This text is from Stanley Hirshson's *General Patton: A Soldier's Life* (New York: Harper Perennial, 2003). The author explores one of the most successful commanders in the history of the U.S. Army, who played a crucial role in World War II. If you were writing a paper on the effect of the war on Patton's life, you might want to include this quote from page 134 of Hirshson's book:

> *Wartime is a career soldier's golden age. In peacetime promotions come slowly, and glory often comes from seeing that your branch of service survives, often at the expense of another branch. With the army small and almost everyone knowing everyone else, the social game often becomes as important as the talent game, and at the first of these Beatrice and George Patton excelled.*

If you wanted to use the above as an extended direct quote, you would record the entire thing on a note card. You might label it "Patton—significance of World War II in life." At the bottom, you'd note the author's last name (Hirshson) and the page on which the quote appears (134).

Sample Note Card for **Quotation**

> ### Patton—significance of World War II in life
>
> " *Wartime is a career soldier's golden age. In peacetime promotions come slowly, and glory often comes from seeing that your branch of service survives, often at the expense of another branch. With the army small and almost everyone knowing everyone else, the social game often becomes as important as the talent game, and at the first of these Beatrice and George Patton excelled.* " *Hirshson, p. 134*

If you wanted to include the entire thing, you would introduce this and then use the quote. Some instructors and style guides call for you to make long quotations—say, of forty words or more—into a block quotation. In other words, it will be offset from the rest of your paper. A space will come before and after it, and it will be indented five spaces. It will be single-spaced. On the next page is an example of how that would look.

Compared to peacetime, World War II gave Patton a chance to demonstrate his leadership and military planning abilities. According to historian Stanley Hirshson,

Wartime is a career soldier's golden age. In peacetime promotions come slowly, and glory often comes from seeing that your branch of service survives, often at the expense of another branch. With the army small and almost everyone knowing everyone else, the social game often becomes as important as the talent game, and at the first of these Beatrice and George Patton excelled.[1]

This number refers the reader to the corresponding number in your footnotes or endnotes, where the source for this information would be given. You will learn more about footnotes and endnotes in chapter 5.

In other words, peacetime could be challenging for a soldier like Patton. It made more use of his social skills than his strategic talents.

You might also choose to use a shorter quote. If you wanted to use just his first sentence, for example, you could do it as shown on the next page.

Even before the war, Patton was a leading figure in the army, but it was through leading men into battle that he proved himself to be a great military commander. In the words of historian Stanley Hirshson, "Wartime is a career soldier's golden age."[1]

Handling Paraphrases

What is a paraphrase? It's a restatement or rewording of a particular passage. You paraphrase when you're not taken enough with the author's words to quote him or her, but you want to follow closely his or her structure or organization of material.[17] You think the point he or she is making is important to your paper and want to present the author's ideas in the same general way he or she did, although you're going to use different words. Often writers paraphrase passages that are complicated or technical, making them easier to understand. Think of this as translating, if you will.[18] When you paraphrase, you should read a passage. Then, look away from the source material while you're writing your paraphrase. When you're done, go back and look at what you've written down in comparison to what the author wrote. Make sure you have not simply written down most of their words, changing just one or two here or there.

It's a good idea to write down a reminder for yourself in your notes to jog your memory later as to how you see your paraphrase fitting into your project. If you want to use a unique term or a particular phrase the author has employed, be sure to use quotation marks to set it apart. Be sure to record the source as well, including the relevant page number.

Sample Note Card for **Paraphrase**

> **Patton—significance of World War II in life** P
>
> Patton's military career took off during the war. Before the war, there wasn't as much opportunity to advance and the main mission was to maintain the army. To succeed during peacetime, a soldier needed social skills as well as military talent. Patton and his wife were especially good at handling the social aspect of the army.
>
> Hirshson, p. 134

If you wanted to use this information in your paper, you would need to make sure to give proper credit to Hirshson, as shown here:

> Even before the war, Patton was an important member of the military. According to historian Stanley Hirshson, Patton and his wife Beatrice thrived in the small social world of the U.S. Army.[1]

Creating Summaries

Some sources you will just want to summarize. *Summarize* comes from the word *sum*. When you sum up something, you get to the gist of it. You condense it. When you summarize or write a summary (sometimes called a *précis*), you take just the essential information or ideas from a passage. You take the main points. You don't want details or explanations. Summaries differ from paraphrases in that they're generally much shorter and focus mostly on facts. They usually record the information an author has presented, rather than his or her ideas or arguments.

How exactly do you summarize? Look at your source. Figure out which facts or ideas are relevant to your paper. Write them down, but in your own words. Use quotation marks if you take down a specific phrase the author used. At times, you will also come across a statistic that you will want to use. In all cases, you must write down the source you're getting your information from!

To illustrate, let's return to the Stanley Hirshson text. The original quote is shown again below, with a sample summary on the next page:

> *Wartime is a career soldier's golden age. In peacetime promotions come slowly, and glory often comes from seeing that your branch of service survives, often at the expense of another branch. With the army small and almost everyone knowing everyone else, the social game often becomes as important as the talent game, and at the first of these Beatrice and George Patton excelled.*
> —*Hirshson, p. 134*

Sample Note Card for **Summary**

Patton—significance of World War II in life   **S**

Before the war, there wasn't as much chance to get promoted.

*Military was a small social circle
To succeed, a soldier needed:*
1) social skills
2) military talent

Patton and wife were good social networkers
                                    Hirshson, p. 134

Bear this in mind: What you need to be able to do above all else is know exactly what you were doing when you recorded a note. Were you quoting, paraphrasing, or summarizing?

Many educators recommend using some sort of system to keep track of what sort of note you are making. Melissa Walker, the author of a book about completing research projects, recommends marking quotations with big quotation marks, paraphrases with a P, and summaries with an S. You might label your own ideas with an M for *me* or *mine*, or with your initials. Other educators advocate using different colors of ink to differentiate between quotations, paraphrases, and your own ideas.

As you go along, do not forget to write down the source and the page number or Web address the information comes from.

How to Take Great Notes

- When you're reading and you come across material that is of use to you, get ready to take notes.

- Decide if you want to quote this material. If the writing itself doesn't really add to your paper, paraphrase it. If there's a whole lot of information you want to digest, summarize it.

- Distinguish between quotations, paraphrases, summaries, and your own ideas in your notes by using a system of your own choosing.

- Include in your notes the information you will need when it comes time to write a citation.

- Save all your notes until after your instructor has graded your paper and given it back to you.[19]

Chapter 5

Putting Together Your Project Using Proper Citations

IN HIGH SCHOOL AS WELL AS COLLEGE, research projects can take different forms. The form in which you present what you have found out will vary from teacher to teacher and class to class. Most often, you'll probably be assigned a research paper. But that's not always the case. Teachers also sometimes ask students to give oral reports or to put together a multimedia presentation on a computer. To create such a presentation, you use multimedia or presentation software, such as Microsoft's PowerPoint®, Adobe® Acrobat® Connect™ Professional, and many others. Multimedia presentations are something like a slide show. They can include not just words and still images, but video and music. They're created and shown on computers. Sometimes they're used to present a story or show art. Usually, however, they present information.

When creating oral reports or multimedia presentations, it's important to follow the same rules you do when doing other academic work. It's very important that you do your own work. The words you use must be your own, or you must indicate that you're using a quotation. When you're giving a speech, you should state outright when you're quoting and whom you're quoting from.

In your speech, you could do this by saying something along the lines of "In the words of . . ." or "So-and-so is considered to be an expert in such-and-such. He believed in such-and-such, as this quote demonstrates: . . ." Then you'd add the quote there.

In multimedia presentations, you can add quotation marks around text, just like you would in a paper. Some people like to add the name of the person they're quoting directly after a quotation, in italics. You can add the title of a book, too, if you want. It's an excellent idea to make the last slide in your multimedia presentation a list of credits. It can be the equivalent of a bibliography. It might also say where you got your images.[1]

Putting Together a Research Project

There are two stages of research projects, after selecting a topic. First, you do the research. Ideally, you will always have enough time to make putting together your project a second, separate stage.

Whenever you research and write at the same time, you greatly increase the risk of committing plagiarism. This is especially true if you're the sort of person who likes to copy and paste material from the Internet. Remember, that's a very dangerous practice. If you do it without giving credit, it could end up getting you kicked out of school or fired from a job.[2] Reflecting on why he got expelled from Great Britain's University of Kent, former student Michael Kent recalled "[I] always used the Internet, cutting and pasting stuff."[3]

Let's presume, however, that you are working on a research project and you've been successful at managing your time. (That's a great accomplishment when you're a busy student.) You have researched until you have enough material to write the required number of pages or speak for the required number of minutes. You've looked back through your outline to double-check that you're going to cover everything you wanted to. Perhaps you realize that your outline was inadequate in some way. There is an aspect of the problem you're considering that you hadn't realized. Maybe you came across some particularly interesting information that's made you shift the focus of your paper. This, actually, is a very good sign. It means you've been doing some thinking on your own. When you do original work, you often have to revise your plan in the middle of a project.[4] The best thing to do in a case like this is go back and

Do's and Don'ts of Plagiarism

DO include quotations you like in your research projects. **DON'T** do so without using quotation marks, saying who wrote or said the words you like, and adding a citation to your footnotes, endnotes, or parenthetical notes. You will learn more about how to do that later in this chapter.

DO paraphrase, especially if you want to prove that other people support your point. **DON'T** do so without a citation!

DO summarize material when you come across a long passage and only want to use its main points. **DON'T** neglect to say you're doing so. Once again, acknowledge it by adding a citation.

DO prepare a bibliography (a list of sources you've consulted) for every research project. **DON'T**, however, list sources you have not in fact used.

revise your outline before beginning to put together your project.

Perhaps you think that when you've reached the end of the research phase, the time has come to begin writing your paper or your speech (or to create the slides in your multimedia presentation). Wait! It is better not to start writing right away. Writing experts advise that you read through all your research notes first. This will help you make sure that you understand all your material. If you find out you do not, you'll either need to talk to your teacher or go do more research. If you've taken your notes on note cards, you can arrange them to reflect the order in which you want to present the information you have collected. If you've taken research notes on your computer, you might want to reorganize them to put them in the best order.

Ideally, you will write your first draft without referring to your research notes.[5] When you're done, you can go back and check to make sure you've got everything right. You should try to be completely familiar with your material before you start to write. It will be much easier for you to write if you are. Write in your own words. Let this idea sink in—for example, the Seattle public schools say you must "[make] sure your own voice is heard."[6] A magazine called *Education World* expands on this concept, telling students, "Use your own words whenever possible. No one expects you to write like an expert or a professional writer." Of course, you shouldn't write in an extremely informal voice. *Education World* goes on to add, "You should . . . write like a serious, intelligent student."[7]

In other words, you should take your time and select precisely the right vocabulary you're looking for. Yet you don't need to feel pressure to use big words. You don't need to sound learned or very educated, like a professor. You can use your own way of talking. In fact, you should try to develop your own writing style. One way to do this is to think about how you would explain what you've been learning or thinking about to a friend or classmate who knew little about it.

If you are clearly using your own words, your teacher will realize that you are not simply repeating what you learned from books written by others. He or she will know you understand what you're talking about. Also bear in mind that one of the clues that tell teachers they are looking at a plagiarized paper is the style. Changes in tone, or the character of writing, for example, are one way they can tell they're looking at a cut-and-paste job.[8] Think about this. Students often write short and straightforward sentences. Professional authors, on the other hand, tend to write longer sentences and use more formal language. Their work will also be more polished. This is something that teachers instantly recognize.

Whether you're writing a term paper or thesis paper, you should concentrate during the first draft on writing about your topic in your own words. As you come to places where you might want to add a quotation or a statistic, you can make a note for yourself. But don't worry about adding them at this point. What you want is to make a rough version of your paper from start to finish.

What Teachers Usually Grade On

- Whether you fulfill the assignment (answer the question the teacher asked)
- Your choice of sources
- The ideas you have had, based on your research
- Additions of useful quotations and paraphrases
- Paraphrasing well
- Citing correctly
- Making smooth transitions between paraphrases, quotations, and your own ideas[9]

Polishing Your Work

When you go back to revise your rough draft, you will want to add supporting material such as quotations and citations. Go back through your notes one more time. Choose which quotations you still want to use. You may find that you have more than enough quotations and that you should actually paraphrase some of the ones you took down during the research note-taking process. Go back through your rough draft to see where you want to add quotations or paraphrased material.[10]

Be careful when you do this. When you want to use a quotation, it's very important to introduce it. You can start out your sentence by saying who you are going to quote. Remember what Stanley Hirshson had to say about General Patton (see chapter 4). You might state your belief that World War II was the pinnacle, or the high point, of his professional life. You can then use Hirshson's words to reinforce what you have to say, like this:

> *During World War II, General George S. Patton was at the pinnacle of his professional life. As the historian Stanley Hirshson has pointed out, "Wartime is a career soldier's golden age."[1]*

You might also want to add to your sentence the title of the work in which the words appeared, for example: As the historian Stanley Hirshson has pointed out in *General Patton: A Soldier's Life,* "Wartime . . ." Check, double-check, even triple-check the quotation to make sure you've got it exactly right, in terms of both words and punctuation.[11] It can be acceptable to change the punctuation or capitalization in a quote in certain cases, but the rules for how to do this properly are complex, so it is best to avoid doing so. If you must, follow the guidelines offered by a style guide.[12] Quotations will require a citation, in the form of a parenthetical note (also referred to as an in-text note), a footnote, or an endnote. Instructions on how to create these will be given shortly.

When you paraphrase someone else's material, it's also very important to state within your actual text—not just in your citation notes—where you got this material. If you want to discuss the point that Hirshson makes regarding Patton's military career, inserting your paraphrase of his material, you have to provide an attribution as well as a citation for that information. You must indicate that he was the one who pointed this out to you. You could introduce your paraphrase with the words: "According to Hirshson, ..." Of course you'll also have to create a citation for the paraphrase. If you want to give a summary of Hirshson's account of Patton's career, on the other hand, you need not give the name of the historian or the name of his book within your main text. Summaries do not need attribution in the text of your paper itself. Like quotes and paraphrases, however, they do usually require a citation note, which will be covered soon.[13]

How to Quote

- Go back through your notes and look at all the quotes you recorded.

- Decide which to use. Choose those with words that are absolutely memorable or that back up the exact point you are trying to make.

- Decide how to use them. Will you use them to introduce your material or back it up?

- Whichever you choose, you must give the source of the quote in your text. So if you want to point out that by the end of the war, Japan was struggling to hold on to scattered outposts, you might want to use a quote and attribute it in the text, as shown on the next page.

*One marine summed up everyone's thoughts
when he said, "Whadda we want with a place
nobody ever heard of before?"[1]*

- Once you've inserted your quote, immediately create the needed footnote or endnote. The citation for the marine's statement would be:

  1. Steinberg, Rafael and the editors of Time-Life Books. Island Fighting. Alexandria, VA: Time-Life Books, 1978, p. 18.

- It's a good idea to include in your bibliography all the sources you quote from.

Citing Sources in Your Citation Notes and Bibliography

Most research papers include a bibliography. That's a general list of the sources you've used. The sources are usually arranged by the author's last name, or if there is no author, by the title. In most cases, books, articles, and Web sites are combined into one list. Some instructors will ask students to break down their bibliography into categories, however, listing books and articles separately.

You also use citation notes to indicate exactly where you've gotten the specific material used in your paper—whether you quote, paraphrase, draw on one source for a summary, or use a fact that's not widely known. This does not refer to your research notes—the written or typed records you made while doing research—but a note that tells your reader the exact source of the information you're presenting.

Such notes can take three different forms. They can be in-text parenthetical references, footnotes, or endnotes. Your instructor will almost certainly tell you what is required, either in hand-outs passed out at the start of the school year or when a particular assignment is made. If not, ask to find out what he or she wants. In-text paren-thetical references appear within the actual text of your paper, in parentheses. They provide the last name of the author of the book you're drawing from and the page number the relevant quotation or information appeared on. Footnotes and endnotes are numbered and appear at the bottom (foot) of the page or at the end of the paper.

Imagine this. You're writing your paper about Patton. You want to talk about the Pattons' social life and use the quote from Hirshson. You could do it like this:

> General Patton worked hard to connect with other military personnel, not just on the job but after work as well. According to historian Stanley Hirshson, "With the army small and almost every-one knowing everyone else, the social game often becomes as important as the talent game, and at the first of these Beatrice and George Patton excelled" (Hirshson, p. 134).

The parenthetical comment would indicate that you got this information from a particular source mentioned in the bibliography. Works that use in-text citations always have bibliographies. Works with footnotes or endnotes usually do, too, although that depends on a publisher's or teacher's requirements.

Creating Citation Notes

Let's borrow some text from earlier in the book that includes a quote, to demonstrate how different types of citation notes might appear in your projects.

Using In-Text Notes

If you wanted to make an in-text citation for the quote, it would appear like this:

> *Paraphrasing is reproducing "the exact sense of a written passage or oral statement in your own words" (Walker, p. 73).* Sense *is the key word there.*

In your bibliography, you would list as one of your sources:

> Walker, Melissa. <u>Writing Research Papers: A Norton Guide</u>. New York: W. W. Norton, 1984.

Using Footnotes

For a footnote, first you need to add a reference number to the main text:

> *Paraphrasing is reproducing "the exact sense of a written passage or oral statement*

in your own words."[1] Sense is the key word there.

Then this footnote would appear at the bottom of the page:

1. Walker, Melissa. <u>Writing Research Papers: A Norton Guide</u>. New York: W. W. Norton, 1984, p. 73.

Using Endnotes

Endnotes are like footnotes, except that they appear at the end of the paper instead of on the bottom of the page. So your paper would look like this:

Paraphrasing is reproducing "the exact sense of a written passage or oral statement in your own words."[1] Sense is the key word there.

Then you would list the citation along with the rest of your notes in the back of your report. Once again, your note for this section would look like this:

1. Walker, Melissa. <u>Writing Research Papers: A Norton Guide</u>. New York: W. W. Norton, 1984, p. 73.

We have used the number 1 for all of our sample citations. But depending on your teacher's requirements, endnotes would be numbered consecutively from the beginning to the end of your paper, or possibly within each chapter or section (starting at number 1 again for the next chapter or section). Footnotes are usually numbered consecutively on each page of your paper, starting at number 1 again for the next page.

Finishing Touches

As you revise your paper, you might want to move material from one section to another. Be careful when you cut and paste. If you are not, you might delete your citation notes by mistake or get confused as to which one goes where. If you decide to add tables, charts, graphs, or illustrations, make sure to add credits for them as well. You could do this in a caption under the graphic material or, in the case of a paper long enough to require a table of contents, make an illustrations list.

When you're done revising, take the time to look back through your footnotes carefully. You may need to check their form against a style guide. Publishers often employ fact checkers to verify that the information presented in books and articles is correct. You might want to do your own fact checking, going back through your notes or photocopies to make sure that you've gotten your dates and facts and figures exactly right and that you've cited the right sources for the right facts.

Your final step is to prepare your bibliography. This will not be hard to do, providing you did a good job and faithfully added sources to your working bibliography. In some cases, teachers will want you to include in your final bibliography just the sources you cited in your notes. In that case, you will need to remove some sources from your working bibliography. In other cases, they will want you to list all the sources you consulted. If your instructor has asked you to provide a selected list of sources, make sure that those you include are the ones you drew on most heavily. Teachers also sometimes ask for annotated bibliographies.[14] This means they want you to add a little bit of description for each source. You might say what a particular book focuses on. You could note if the author of a particular book has a special point of view or a work seems biased. Instructors especially concerned about trying to prevent plagiarism often ask for annotated bibliographies.

Here's one final piece of advice: If you have trouble finishing a paper on time, it's best to talk to your teacher. He or she might be willing to extend your deadline. If the teacher cannot or will not, remember that it is far better to turn in a paper that you have not worked on enough than to turn in a paper you've plagiarized. The difference will be seen in your grade (compare a seventy-five, say, to a zero). It might impact your future, too, as being charged with plagiarism can have other severe consequences, including suspension or expulsion from school. It is worth it to take the time to do your paper right!

Chapter 6

The Fair Use of Illustrations and Photos

IT DOES NOT MATTER whether a student is putting together a research paper for school, a column for a club newsletter, or an entry on his or her blog. You are expected to come up with some of your own ideas and words—and when you use someone else's, you need to give them credit. The same is true when using art or photos. Some people have artistic talent and can create impressive artwork or take beautiful photographs for their school projects. But many individuals aren't skilled enough to be great artists. When most people need an illustration, they must use other people's artwork. To be fair, this means they have to credit them. The bottom line is that they must never present another's artwork as their own.

Can a student buy a drawing at an art show or download a photo from the Internet and then submit it to a contest as his own work? The answer is no. Obviously, that would be cheating. Very few people stoop to this. But there are many, many people who use art unfairly without realizing it.

Using Art in School Research Projects

Perhaps you're working on a paper on the history of the Golden Gate Bridge. During your research, you come across books that include drawings and photos of the bridge. They help you understand exactly how the bridge was built. When you are in such a situation, feel free to photocopy illustrations that will help you write your paper. Take the time to write down where you copy each illustration from. There are two reasons to write down where your pictures come from. First of all, you'll be able to go back to the book later if you need to. And if you decide you want to include that illustration in your paper, you'll be able to provide a credit for it. In other words, you can tell your teacher where you found the illustration.

What if you are doing Internet research? In that case, it is fair for you to print out an image. You can also download images onto your computer. Once again, however, it's important for you to keep track of where you get your pictures. If you print out an entire Web page, the Web address—or URL— should automatically appear at the bottom. (If it does not appear, write it on the printout yourself.) If you decide to print only a photo, you will need to write down the URL. Keep in mind that if you download an image, you cannot use it on your own Web page unless you get permission. There will be more information on how to obtain permissions in chapter 9.

In many cases, when you're working on a research project, it's a great idea to look for relevant pictures to help you understand your topic. You

Clip Art

Clip art refers to collections of images that graphic artists have created especially to be used by other people. They do not specify how the images are to be used. There is free clip art available on the Internet. Also, disks or books of clip art can be bought or borrowed from a library. Your librarian can probably help you find clip art for any project.[1]

may want to include them in your research project as well. They can help your teacher understand what you're talking about. For some assignments, instructors actually may require students to provide illustrations. This is especially true when the assignment is to create a multimedia presentation. In other cases, you may decide on your own to provide an illustration. Maybe you're doing a paper on the Impressionist painter Claude Monet. He made dozens of paintings of haystacks. You might decide in your paper to compare two. You want to try to show why Monet painted the same subject over and over again. In this case, it would be good to include photocopies of the paintings you're discussing.

Claude Monet made more than 20 paintings of haystacks. You may want to include photos of a few—with proper credit—in a paper that compares the different versions.

Sometimes you might want to use a chart, graph, or table in a project. These can be a very effective way to present data, especially if you want to make comparisons. Perhaps you will be reading a book or looking at a Web site and find the perfect graph, for example, to use in your paper. For school, it is all right for you to photocopy or print out what you have found. You must, however, keep track of where you found it so that you can give credit. Other times, you will find information that you can use to make your own chart or graph. Again, you can use this information. But you must note where you got your data.

For a student to add illustrations and photos to a research project is entirely acceptable under the fair use guidelines in copyright law. When you include a copy of a painting, a photograph, or other illustration in a project, there are different ways in which you can provide credits. One way is to include them in captions. A caption is the text that appears under an illustration in a book, magazine, newspaper, or Web page. It can be used to comment on the illustration and to provide a credit line. In the case of most student papers, you can keep the style of your credit line simple. You can indicate the author, title of the book, and page number, or the Web site name and address from which you took the illustration. Another way is to make a credit list for your illustrations. You might want to insert this list right before your bibliography.

If you do decide to make your own chart or graph, give it a title. Underneath, make a credit line that notes where you got your data. This will let your readers know the source of your data. They'll be able to go and look it up themselves, if they need more information.

In and Out of Art Class

Students often create artwork in school. Many schools offer art, photography, and multimedia classes. In art class, sometimes teachers assign their students the task of copying a painting. They also might ask students to bring in photos on which to base a painting. Even though schools stress the importance of doing original work, this

Forgery!

Sometimes artists are found guilty of using their talent for criminal purposes. Forgers make fake artworks that they try to pass off as real. In 1995, a painter named John Myatt went to jail for having sold two hundred paintings that looked just like works by Vincent van Gogh and Marc Chagall. People paid huge sums of money for them. Today, he still makes paintings that look like they were done by famous painters, but he changes some details, such as putting a sofa where an armchair was in the original. And now he openly admits they're fakes.[2]

is one situation in which it's perfectly all right to copy. Copying art has long been part of art education. But, as always, students must not hide the fact that this is what they're doing—copying.

What if you're assigned to do a painting on your own? In that case, you should talk it over with your teacher in advance if you want to copy something you've seen, perhaps in a book or on a magazine cover. In general, your artwork should reflect your own ideas, not someone else's. This is true whether you're in class or you're one of the many students for whom art is a hobby. There are, however, many cases in which artists are inspired by the work of others. They might build on others' ideas, taking them in a new direction. They might paint a scene made famous by a painter, but do it from a different perspective, for example. Students cannot, however, directly copy a famous work.

Art Issues

There are some very interesting issues facing artists. In the past, professional artists often used images from popular culture. The artist Andy Warhol, for example, made art that looked just like a box of Brillo® scrubbers or a Campbell's® soup can. Today, however, major corporations often guard their trademarks—the names or symbols that identify their products—very closely. (Trademarks, copyrights, and patents are further discussed in a sidebar in this chapter.) Thus, Harlequin Enterprises Limited, a book publisher, has taken steps to prevent the painter Natalka Husar from making paintings of romance novel covers. The toy manufacturer Mattel didn't like it when the photographer Tom Forsythe took photographs of Barbie® dolls without its approval.[3] Collage artists, or people who make works of art of many different images, like to include popular culture images in their work and are sometimes challenged by trademark or copyright holders. How does this apply to students? It matters if they're making art that they want to sell on eBay or in a gallery, even if it's in a small town. But it's okay if they use these images for school or personal use—they just can't use them to make money.

Sometimes artists are accused of copying other people's artwork, infringing on a copyright rather than on a trademark. For example, a very successful glass artist named Dale Chihuly filed a copyright lawsuit in Seattle in 2006. For a long time, Chihuly himself blew glass. Today, he still designs glass pieces. However, due to an injury, he

Copyrights, Trademarks, and Patents

Often Americans are confused about the differences between copyrights, trademarks, and patents. Copyrights apply to literary, dramatic, musical, and artistic works. They have to do with the creators' rights to control how their work is used and reproduced. So J. K. Rowling's copyright means she gets to say how her character Harry Potter is used. Trademarks are symbols and names used by companies to distinguish their products from similar products produced by other companies. Coca-Cola® and Coke®, Pepsi®, and Dr Pepper® are registered trademarks. Patents protect the rights of an inventor, granting him or her the sole right for a period of time to make and sell their invention. Thus Nike® has a patent to the technology used to make its Air™ line of shoes. Nintendo® has patents on the Wii™.

has to employ other glassblowers to make the fantastic pieces he imagines. Chihuly has a very interesting style. He is often inspired by the sea, and his pieces look like ocean creatures. They're very striking, especially when he mounts hundreds of them to a floor or ceiling. In his lawsuit, Chihuly has charged that another glass artist was copying his work. Bryan Rubino countersued, arguing that he is not the only one with the right to make what looks like a sea anemone out of glass.[4] Eventually the case was settled out of court.

Photographers also sometimes complain about their work being stolen. The advent of digital photography and the Internet has created big changes for them. Sometimes photographers take a photo and allow it to go up on a Web site, only to discover that suddenly it's seemingly everywhere. People frequently infringe on photographers' rights, not understanding that someone owns the copyright to that cute puppy photo a friend attached to an e-mail this morning. You are also not supposed to alter a photograph without the photographer's consent. This means that you can't use a computer paint program to cut a face from one photo to add to another—unless you took both photographs. You also can't take someone else's photo and "morph" it or change its colors if you intend to profit from it.

As well as protecting their own rights, photographers also have to concern themselves with the rights of others. Commercial photographers have to obtain what are called releases from the models they photograph. In many countries, including the United States, the law says that you also cannot sell photographs taken of ordinary people—if they're readily identifiable—unless you've gotten their okay. There are also privacy laws that affect the work of those who photograph celebrities.

Using Art in a Publication

Some students like to work on publications outside of the classroom. You might work for your school newspaper or on the yearbook. Maybe you belong to a club that publishes a newsletter of some sort. Perhaps you publish a zine—a magazine or newsletter of which just a few copies are printed—or an e-zine, an online magazine. From time to time, you might want to use artwork in your publication. If you yourself have produced the artwork, that's perfectly all right. You can also use clip art. Clip art was created especially for use by publishers, designers, and others, in publications and on Web sites. It's available on the Internet. There are books and CDs available for purchase or to check out from your library. And you can use art that is in the public domain. That's largely art that was created before about 1920.

But what if you want to use something by a contemporary artist or photographer? In that case, if your publication is for sale, you will need to get permission. So without permission, your yearbook

Fair Use and Fan Art

Many students have heard of fan art. That's when an artist takes a popular character from a comic book and makes art using that figure. Most fan art features a character from manga, which are Japanese comic books or graphic novels. Go to any Internet search engine. Type in "Trigun fan art" as search terms. Thousands of links will probably appear.

Is it fair to make fan art? Yes, as long as individuals do it just for their own satisfaction. They can also show such art to other fans. Not only can they show it to friends, but they can send it in to a popular magazine named *Shonen Jump* that holds fan art contests. Video game manufacturers and comic book publishers also often invite fans to submit fan art to their Web sites. What fans cannot do is sell their fan art. Under U.S. copyright law, no one can profit off someone else's work.

cannot include a news photo of the earth-shaking event that occurred your senior year, for example. You also cannot include a funny syndicated comic strip without first getting approval from the creator. The reason these images are off-limits is that they're copyrighted. Their creators get to control how and when they're reproduced. In chapter 9, you'll learn how to ask for permission when you want to use copyrighted materials.

You might also run into this problem if you contribute material to a magazine, for example. Say you've written a review of the alternative rock band Green Day's concert. The editor of your local newspaper or music magazine has expressed interest in it. In such a case, you would be able to submit for publication the photo you took at the concert. But you cannot scan the cover of one of the band's CDs and send that in. To publish that, the publisher would have to apply for permission from the band's recording company.

Using Art on Web Sites

Many students use a Web site or blog as a way of publishing their writings, photographs, and other artwork and information. The rules for using art on Web pages are much like those for using art in publications. Of course, you can post art that is your own creation. But without permission, you cannot simply take an image from another Web site and post it on your own. This is true of images you find on individuals' Web sites as well as those you find on company sites.

While it is simple to download images from a Web site, it is unethical for you to repost material from another person's Web site without permission.

What's more, it's illegal. And the owners of some copyrighted works try very hard to ensure that their stuff is not stolen. This is especially true of the companies that produce popular television shows and movies. Movie production companies, television networks, and record production companies all have special programs that allow them to quickly search the Internet for artwork to which they own the copyright or license. When they find work that has been posted without their permission, they send the Webmaster a notice that they believe there's been a copyright infringement. If the Webmaster doesn't respond by taking down the artwork in question, there could be legal trouble.

Look at Web pages you like to visit, and you'll realize that many Web page designers are not careful. You'll see many sites with images that don't have a permission line. Do not make this mistake. If you have a Web site, follow the rules. If you see artwork you like on the Web, ask for permission to reuse it. In many cases, some people and companies do allow their images to be reproduced at no charge. Once you have a permission letter in hand, usually all you have to do is add a credit line to your Web page. Then you'll be able to post a scan of that cover from your favorite magazine or CD.

Reproductions

When can you reproduce someone else's artwork without permission? The fair use clause in U.S.

copyright law allows people to photocopy pictures for research purposes. That means you can make photocopies for use in a class project. But it also means that you can photocopy images if you're just plain interested in something. Maybe you like a certain kind of car, or perhaps you're interested in a particular designer or sports star. It's okay for you to collect photocopies of images relating to them that appear in print or on the Web. You can keep them in a folder and study, say, the various BMX bikes available or how the covers of the Harry Potter books change from one edition to another.

Many other uses are off-limits, however. You cannot scan the Harry Potter book covers and then print out the scans to sell them. What if you're at a flea market or garage sale and find a great vintage postcard of the Beatles? You can buy it, and you will own that particular postcard. Someone else owns the copyright to that great photo of the Beatles, and someone owns the copyright to the postcard. And thus, you can't reproduce either the postcard or the photo. Remember, you cannot copy photos you didn't take, unless you have permission. It doesn't matter if the photographer is an amateur or a professional. So if a friend has purchased a celebrity photo, you cannot take it to a machine that duplicates photographs and run one off for yourself.

Another thing you cannot do is create merchandise using someone else's art without permission.

So you cannot print T-shirts with someone else's photo of the Statue of Liberty or an illustration that was created for a school theater program. You cannot suddenly decide to have a thousand postcards printed with a photo you saw in Car and Driver or Wired magazine.[5]

Downloading Art

The Internet is a tremendous resource for finding art. In the past, you might have had to go through many books about Frida Kahlo to find a particular painting by her. Today, museums, scholars, and art admirers are taking advantage of the Web and posting images of their favorite paintings and photographs. They also upload photographs of other types of art, including posters, sculptures, and architectural designs.

While modern technology makes it possible to look at artwork that's seldom seen, it is important to remember that the art is not automatically free for the taking. You should feel free to download photographs of your favorite Kahlo paintings, and you can save them to refer back to later. These images can be used as your computer wallpaper or screensaver or printed out to decorate your room, your locker, or a scrapbook. But know that you should not circulate them via e-mail or post them on your own Web site or use them to make a profit in any way.

Chapter 7

The Fair Use of Music and Sound

MANY STUDENTS LISTEN TO MUSIC every day. They also often copy music. If they're in a band, they might photocopy sheet music. More often, teenagers—just like adults—want to copy a recording. In other words, they want to duplicate a favorite song to listen to. They might do that by downloading a tune from the Internet—copying it, in other words, onto their computer. Or they might use their computer or a CD writer to "burn" a mixed CD. Occasionally, teenagers also want to make an original recording of music. What's the difference between copying music and recording it? You record music when you sing a song into a tape recorder, for example. And you copy music when you burn a CD of all your favorite television theme songs.

Occasionally, students want to use music or sound in a project for school. Maybe they're doing an oral report for an American history class and

Musicians and music fans have to follow certain rules to avoid copyright infringement.

want to play a recording of a song popular during the 1930s or a sound clip from a news broadcast. In a music appreciation class, they might want to play a sampling of songs that influenced the rock legend Elvis Presley or the more modern hip-hop duo OutKast.

Students want to use music outside of class, too. Sometimes it's while they are engaged in an extracurricular activity, like with a club or at a big ball game. Probably music is a big part of their lives at home, too. They may even play an instrument and want to be in a band or to record their own versions of famous songs. There are different rules for playing or recording copyrighted music and lyrics outside of educational purposes. In most of these cases, a person has to obtain permission from the individuals and companies that hold the copyrights to the music. Even when creating original music, there are issues that every young musician or songwriter should be aware of.

In all areas of life, it's important for students to keep in mind which ways of using music and sound are fair. It's especially important to understand why it's illegal to download some music and how to avoid doing so.

Music Rights

Under U.S. law, music is protected by two forms of copyright.[1] When a piece of music is written down, it gets what is called a song or musical work

From time to time, you might want to include a sound clip in a project you're working on for school, such as an oral presentation, a multimedia presentation, or a Web page design. This could be just a few bars of music from a CD. But it could also be a recording of just a little something from the radio—a bit of the news, for example. Sometimes people want to use a few seconds of a speech.

To use a sound clip in a commercial production, such as on a CD or on your own personal Web site, would require permission. But you are allowed to use a clip when the purpose is educational. In many cases, you will be able to create your own, using a tape recorder, for example, to record a radio program or homemade sound effects. There are CDs of sound effects available for purchase as well.

You can also use software, such as Windows Media Player, that comes already installed on most new laptops and personal computers to search for audio clips. Or you can do an Internet search to find them. Just use "free sound clip" as your search terms. Be sure to read the copyright and permissions statements on the links you find. Remember to take notes on your sources and include them in your project.

Bear in mind that it's not ethical to alter a sound clip. So you're not supposed to add words to the president's latest radio address and try to fool people into thinking he said something he did not. So if you're writing a spoof of a news conference as a skit to perform for a theater class, for example, you can include an authentic sound clip. Just don't alter it.

copyright. The songwriter establishes copyright just by writing the notes on a piece of blank sheet music or recording it on a tape, for example. If that music gets published as sheet music or in a book of songs, it's usually not the person who wrote the song who registers the copyright but the music publisher. Remember, it is copyright registration that gives a person or company the right to sue for copyright infringement, under U.S. law.

When music is played and recorded on a tape or DVD—as opposed to just being written down on paper—a second copyright is established. That's called the sound recording copyright, and it's usually registered by a record company. It's against the law to violate either the song or the sound recording copyrights. Thus, every time a musician wants to record a song that he or she did not write, he or she may have to get multiple permissions, or licenses.

For example, an artist wants to record a copyrighted song that has already been recorded. Blues singer and musician Ray Charles did that with country music legend Hank Williams's song "Your Cheatin' Heart" in 1962. Charles's version of the song was one of his biggest hits. This was less than ten years after Williams also had a hit with the song himself. More than thirty other singers have also recorded "Your Cheatin' Heart." To do so, they had to get a license. (Another example of a song that has been "covered" many times is "Tainted Love.")

Don't forget the basic principles that should guide you whenever and whatever you write. Your work should be original. Whenever you base your work on an effort by someone else, you need to acknowledge that fact. Under U.S. copyright law, the way musicians acknowledge the debt they owe to other songwriters or musicians is by acquiring licenses.

There have been some very famous court cases involving music rights. In 1970, for example, George Harrison became the first member of the rock group The Beatles to have a hit record on his own. His song "My Sweet Lord" climbed to the top of the charts and made him lots of money. But another band named The Chiffons had recorded a song called "He's So Fine" in 1963. Listeners realized that Harrison had used the hook, or the notes that lead into a song, from "He's So Fine" in "My Sweet Lord." The Chiffons' music publisher sued. In 1976, a judge found Harrison guilty of "unconscious plagiarism." In other words, he decided that Harrison had heard The Chiffons' song. Somehow that musical phrase had stuck in his head. Without realizing what he was doing, he copied The Chiffons. For this, he had to pay millions of dollars.[2] Harrison expressed regret for what he had done.

If a filmmaker wants to use Ray Charles's recording of Hank Williams's "Your Cheatin' Heart" in a movie, then he or she would have to get permission from both the holder of the song copyright—

Williams's heirs or his publishing company—and Ray Charles's record label, since it's Charles's recording being used. If a rapper wanted to sample even just a few bars of the same recording, he or she would be in the same situation, needing two licenses to do so. Obviously, this can get very complicated.

Musicians also have to get licenses to perform songs live, to produce what are called derivative works, or to distribute copies of a recording to the public.[3] The law also forbids the rental of CDs and other recordings. The recording industry lobbied for this law to protect the rights of recording labels. This is why Blockbuster stores, for example, don't have them. Libraries can allow them to be checked out because they do not profit from doing so.

Copying Music

When is it legal to copy music? We're no longer talking about recording live music, making a tape or CD of a band as it plays. Now we're considering making a duplicate of printed sheet music or of an existing recording.

Let's talk first about photocopying sheet music. In most cases, you can make one photocopy of a song out of a school textbook or a library book, so that you yourself can play it at home. But you're not supposed to buy a piece of sheet music and then copy it for every member of your band. Also, if you ever want to reproduce a piece of copyrighted

Derivative Works

To understand what a derivative work is, you must first learn the meaning of the word *derive*. It means "to come from." A derivative work is one that's based on another and uses its main ideas. Derivative works include movies based on books or musical works based on classical music themes, such as a famous melody. They also include translations and fictionalizations, meaning a work of fiction—such as a novel or screenplay—that's based on an actual event. A condensation, or a shortened version of a longer work, is also considered a derivative work.

In terms of music, one song that's based on another is considered a derivation. So if you wanted to make a recording of a song written by someone else that you had rewritten for your band, this would require permission from the songwriter or music publishing company that had registered the copyright to the original song. You also can't take a well-known tune and write new words to go along with it, even for educational purposes. That's considered a derivative work, which is a copyright infringement.[4]

music in a student magazine or on a Web site, that's going to require permission because that would also make it available to a number of people. Now let's consider lyrics. Those are the words to songs. They are covered by song copyrights, too. So you can't make a large number of copies of them or put them up on your Web page without permission. Even with permission, you want to make sure to provide credit for the creator and copyright holder.

What can you do with a CD you buy? If you buy it, you have the right to play it for your own personal enjoyment. You can play it all you like at home or on the road, whether you're alone, with your family, or in a small group of friends.[5] You're also allowed to copy that CD for yourself. Many personal computers and laptops are now capable of copying music off one CD and burning it onto a blank CD. To do this, you can use a media player, which is a computer software program. Media players come on many new computers. It's perfectly fine for you to do this, for example, to make a second CD to take on a trip, whether you're just going for a short ride in the car or heading off to Australia for a year.

You're also allowed to copy the CD into another format. So if you want to listen to your new music but not on a CD player, you are entitled to copy it into another format. Some people still use tape recorders. They play their CD and record it onto an audiotape. Many more people transfer music from a CD to an MP3 player.

One thing you are not supposed to do is copy music for another person, even a friend or family member. You may loan your CD to a friend so he or she can listen to it. But your friend shouldn't copy it. And you shouldn't borrow a friend's CD and copy it for yourself. You also aren't allowed to copy a CD so that it can be played as part of a public performance—during a play or at a pep rally, for example. (You also can't play the CD you purchased unless you have permission.) You can't copy a song to add to a CD that holds a slideshow of digital photos if you're later going to copy that CD and give it away.

Illegal copying may not seem like such a big deal on a case-by-case basis. What record producers

You are not supposed to copy music for another person, even a friend or family member.

and musicians would say, however, is that there's widespread copying going on. For example, if one hundred people make just one copy for a friend, then the record company—and the musicians they pay royalties to—has lost the money from all of those copies. But there is an even bigger problem with music piracy. This is when people copy CDs and sell them—that's the important point, they make money from them—usually for less than the recording company. The record company, music publishing company, recording artist, and songwriter all lose money when people buy illegal copies instead of legitimate ones.

Illegal copies of CDs are nearly everywhere. Go on eBay or to a flea market in any big American city. You'll probably see pirated CDs for sale. American CDs are also regularly ripped off and pirated for sale in the many other countries in which American music is popular. In Mexico, you can buy an illegal copy of a CD by a top American artist for just under $2.[6] (Illegal copies account for 65 percent of music sales in Mexico.) In China, millions of pirated CDs are sold every year.[7] People buy them because of their cheap price. But one reason to avoid buying pirated CDs—aside from the fact that it's absolutely unethical and illegal to do so—is that they're likely to be of very poor quality.

Today, music piracy has become such a problem that it's investigated by hundreds of law enforcement agencies in the United States as well as in other parts of the world. Both the Federal Bureau of Investigation (FBI) and the Immigration and Customs Enforcement agency have become involved. In November of 2005, for example, an FBI search of a store outside Detroit turned up more than ten thousand pirated CDs.[8]

Why should you care about music piracy? Think about how you would feel if you were a musician—or the company that was trying to promote a musician. You would certainly want to make the money you deserved for the work you did. You would be angry if someone ripped off your CD, paying you absolutely nothing.

Recognizing a Pirated CD

The Recording Industry Association of America has a few tips for how to spot a pirated CD:

- Check the price. If it's extremely low, the CD is likely an illegal copy.

- Look at the cover. Genuine CDs have bar codes and often the name of a recording company and its address.

- Read the cover. Look for misspellings. Check to see if the cover art is blurry instead of bright and clear.

- Make sure the CD is shrink-wrapped and that the plastic is not very loose.

- When you listen to pirated CDs, the sound quality is often bad.[9]

Downloading Music

Today it's very easy to download music from the Internet. There are plenty of places to download music legally as well as illegally. But downloading music is a relatively new phenomenon. It was first done on a large scale in 1999, when a Web site called Napster was established.

Napster was the first major peer-to-peer (P2P) file-sharing tool. It made it possible for people to share their MP3 music files. Some users uploaded songs to the Web site, which Napster indexed and made available to the public. Other users downloaded the songs, meaning they didn't have to buy a CD to listen to the latest hit. Eventually, Napster was sued by the RIAA for copyright infringement. When the court decided in favor of the RIAA, the Web site shut down for a time. In 2004, the relaunched

The Napster Case

The technology behind Napster enabled users to make their MP3 files available to others. Its software allowed for the indexing and searching of MP3 files. Most files resided on users' computers, although some were ultimately uploaded to Napster servers. Napster made it possible for users to search for copies of the music they wanted and then transfer them to their own computers over the Internet.

While its software made it easy to share music, it wasn't legal. Napster was the first P2P file-sharing network to get sued. The company was charged with copyright infringement by the Recording Industry Association of America (RIAA). The court ruled in the RIAA's favor, saying that Napster had infringed its distribution rights when it uploaded file names and its reproduction rights when it allowed for distribution of music files.

Napster started to sell legal downloads.[10] Today it's one of many Web sites where users can pay to legally download songs.

The Napster case hardly brought illegal downloading to an end. Other sites allowing illegal downloading continued to pop up, despite the fact that the RIAA and other organizations were prepared to fight them. In 2005, a court found that the hosts of file-sharing networks could be held liable for encouraging users to infringe on copyrights. In the summer of 2006, an extremely popular site called Kazaa settled with the RIAA, agreeing to pay a fine of what was reported to be $100 million.[11] While illegal downloading began to decrease, legal downloads of music began to increase. In 2003, Apple, the company that manufactures the Macintosh computer and the iPod, launched iTunes.[12]

Legal Downloading

Today, there are many places where you can legally download music. Downloading remains very popular. One study shows that there's been a decrease in illegal downloading by 20 percent since 2004.[13] Today, most people realize that taking music off the Internet without payment or permission is wrong. In fact, 80 percent of Americans say illegal downloading is a form of stealing, and 92 percent say they've never done it.[14] Legal downloading, on the other hand, is on the increase. In 2004, users downloaded 55 million songs during a six-month period. In 2005, the number was 158 million.[15]

Most people are probably familiar with commercial music Web sites. The most popular is probably iTunes, but Walmart.com and Yahoo! Music are other very successful sites. One thing many may not realize, however, is that there are several other legal sources of music to download. One is musicians' Web sites. Many local bands upload their songs specifically so that fans can download them. They find this is a good way to generate excitement about their music and hope that it will get more people to buy their CDs. You can also find download links on MySpace or by doing an Internet search.

Just make sure you read a site's fine print to ensure what you're doing is legal. In many cases, of course, there will be no fine print to read. Lots of people who put up Web sites aren't trustworthy or are unaware of copyright issues. If you have doubts, don't download! Also, you're not supposed to upload copyrighted songs to play on your MySpace page.

Some Signs a Downloading Site May be Illegal

1. It does not charge a fee.

2. The songs it is offering for free are currently available for sale at stores such as Wal-Mart or Best Buy.

3. It uses peer-to-peer technology, meaning you're getting a song from another individual rather than from a company or a band.

4. It includes text talking about why copyright laws should not be obeyed.

Recording Music

There are lots of computer programs as well as tape recorders and other devices that let you record music. Clearly, you are allowed to record a song that you yourself have written. But can you legally record— meaning taping or burning a CD of your band

Always make sure that you download music legally.

playing—your own version of someone else's song? The answer is almost always yes. However, in some cases permission—and sometimes a payment—will be required.

You can record anything that's in the public domain. There are many songs on which the copy-

Lyrics

There's a lot of misinformation out there concerning how people are allowed to use lyrics. Many people mistakenly believe that it's all right to use just a line or two from a song on their Web site or in a book. This is wrong. It doesn't matter how much of a song is used. There are certain rules that must be followed.

When you're working on a school project, you should feel free to use lyrics. Just follow the regular rules for citing the source where you found them. But beware if what you want to do is use them on your Web site. You can only do this if you have permission from the music publisher. Also, if you write your own music, remember that you can't use another's lyrics in your own songs without permission.

Organizations and companies, as well as individuals, have to watch out for how they use lyrics. In 2004, the rapper Eminem sued the Apple Computer company after it released an ad in which a boy sang a little of the lyrics from one of his songs.[16] A Web site called International Lyrics Server had to close down because it was posting lyrics without permission.[17]

right has expired. Today, copyright is automatically established as soon as a song is either written down or recorded. This was not true in the past, however, and there are plenty of songs for which the copyright was never registered.

Also, there are cases in which songwriters choose to let others have free access to their compositions. Sometimes those are new songs written by songwriters who still register their copyright, while choosing to grant some rights to the public under what's called a Creative Commons license.[18] An artist or composer might choose the Creative Commons license that allows users to download their work from the Internet but not to change it or include it on a Web site, for example, that's going to make money. There are five other variations on this—the most liberal allows other users to distribute, remix, and add to a work in any way, as long as credit is given to the original creator.

But there are also some very popular songs that people assume are in the public domain, when this is not actually the case. One notable example is "Happy Birthday to You."[19] It's not against the law for people to sing happy birthdays at parties. But what is illegal is for it to be used in a movie, TV program, or play or for a manufacturer to manufacture a toy that plays the tune unless they pay royalties. Almost all contemporary music is copyrighted. One way you can find out for sure if a CD is copyrighted is by looking at the case for the copyright symbol © and date in the fine print.

A librarian could also help you find out if a specific song is under copyright.

What if you want to record a previously unrecorded (untaped) copyrighted song? That could mean a song that one of your friends has written or a song for which the sheet music is available, but which no one has recorded yet. That just requires permission from the copyright holder—your friend or the music publisher. But what about recording a song that's already been a big hit on the radio? That does require permission. What's interesting— perhaps even confusing—is that the copyright owner is required to give it to you. It involves what is called a compulsory license. That's too complicated to explain here. But the law says anybody who wants it is "entitled" to record the music. Yes, they must ask for permission. But it must also be given.

What would happen if a big-name band wanted to make a CD, recording a new song they'd heard a local band play but which hadn't been recorded yet? They can only do so if they get permission. What happens if the same big-name band wanted to cover a Beatles song that had been recorded? They'd have to get a compulsory license, just as the garage band would if it decided to cover "Yellow Submarine."

The easiest way for you to find out whom to contact for permission for a song that's already been recorded is to check the liner notes, which are in the booklet that comes with the CD. They will say who holds the song and recording copyrights.

Sampling and the Law

Since hip-hop music developed, its artists have liked to sample. Hip-hop sampling began when DJs spun popular records, playing just their favorite fragments.[20] Then musicians started appropriating, or incorporating, little bits of other people's music into their own recordings. Hip-hop artists became involved in a legal conflict over appropriation for the first time in 1979, when the Sugar Hill Gang recorded their song "Rapper's Delight." It included an instrumental line from the 1970s disco group Chic's number-one hit "Good Times," which had reached the top of the pop chart earlier that year. The Sugar Hill Gang did not have a DJ in the studio to play the Chic record. Instead, the studio's house band performed the instrumental parts. Still, the people who had written "Good Times" sued. The lawsuit was settled out of court. The Sugar Hill Gang admitted its guilt and agreed to pay for the use of the music.

By the mid-1980s, other hip-hop artists were being sued for sampling. Sampling is when bands and performers include a little bit of someone else's recording or play a little bit of someone else's song on their own recording. In 1986, Def Jam Recordings got sued when the Beastie Boys used Jimmy Castor's trademark line "Yo, Leroy" from his song "The Return of Leroy (Part One)." In 1990, David Bowie and Freddie Mercury sued Vanilla Ice for using the bass line and piano riffs from their song "Under Pressure." Both of these cases were settled out of court. In 1991, a judge ruled that Biz Markie had violated Gilbert O'Sullivan's rights when he used some recorded accompaniment to "Alone Again (Naturally)" without permission.[21] After that, hip-hop artists began to get licenses for the samples they used. Puff Daddy (now known as Diddy) paid big bucks—perhaps even $1 million or more—to sample songs by Led Zeppelin and The Police. One hip-hop historian has written that "[Puff Daddy] has repeatedly expressed admiration for the materials he uses, but he also seems proud of the fact that he can afford to use them."[22]

Today, hip-hop artists continue to sample, and sampling remains a subject of controversy. Those who do so are on one of two extremes. They're often either already established and are making enough money to pay for the licenses, or they're so new that they're hoping not to get caught doing illegal sampling. Most record labels now employ people whose job it is to listen to other recordings to see if their stuff is being stolen.[23] It's interesting to note that there have been cases rappers have won. When Roy Orbison's publishing company sued 2 Live Crew for reworking "Pretty Woman," for instance, the Supreme Court ruled that this could be considered a parody—a funny takeoff on the song—and thus it was decided to be a fair use.[24] More legal cases about sampling are likely to occur, as there are no clear guidelines for it under current copyright laws.

Public Performance of Music

Did you know that it's illegal for your school's cheer-leaders to perform to popular music at a game? That's right. They can only do that if the school has purchased a license. There are vendors, or companies, who sell licenses to royalty-free music.[25] You can find them by doing an Internet search using the phrase "royalty-free music" or asking a librarian.

The same applies to talent shows, plays, and the like. This includes singing a song in a nightclub, playing a song at halftime, playing a CD at a fund-raiser or over a business intercom system, broadcasting a performance of a song, and retransmitting a broadcast.[26] Webcasts and audio streaming are also regulated.

Similarly, the law gives performance rights to the owners of the copyright on plays and choreographed dances. So every time you want to perform a musical, you're going to need to get permission from the company that owns its copyright, the Dramatists Play Service. Every time your school's theater director decides to put on a copy-righted play, he or she has to purchase scripts and pay for performance rights.[27] And your local dance company will have to apply for permission from the choreographer or the agency that represents him if it wants to perform his recent choreograph of a famous ballet.

Chapter 8

The Fair Use of Video, Computer Software, and Other Media

ALONG WITH WORDS, ART, AND MUSIC, students also need to handle video and other types of media, such as computer software and video games, with care. In school, they might want to use a video in a class project. Some students might even have a chance to earn school credit for a short movie they make. More commonly, students will want to download software to use in a computer class.

Outside of school, there are also many occasions when students want to use media. Students regularly use computers at home and at the library. Some may even use computers in an Internet cafe. Issues arise not just when they go to download videos or games, but when they create Web pages or post blogs.

Some students learn how to operate a video camera to use it for school projects.

Using Video at School

From time to time, you may get to use video as part of a class project. Perhaps you'll be assigned to create a multimedia presentation about how television portrays drug use or on the events leading to the end of World War II. It's recently become possible to find video clips easily on the Internet. Such search engines as Google have made it possible for users to search just for videos. Many legal downloading services have movies and video clips for sale. In some cases, there are free video clips available on company sites. Movie and television production companies make trailers available, for instance. Sports teams might make video clips available. Sites such as YouTube feature many video clips made by amateurs. Be warned, however, that to figure out which are legal to download, you have to read the fine print. If there isn't any fine print, you should assume that the videos are illegal. When in doubt, don't download.

When you find a clip you like, it's easy to download it. In many cases, you can just use the Download button on the site. Be ready to wait. It can take a very long time for video to download, depending on the speed of your Internet connection.

Filmmaking

Perhaps you're taking a filmmaking class or filmmaking is your hobby. Maybe you've saved up and bought a used video camera. You're working on a screenplay for a radio/television/film class or on a short for a young filmmakers' competition. Lots of teenagers contribute films to YouTube and Web sites like it.

What do you need to be thinking about? First, let's consider scripts. Who's qualified to write a script? J. Michael Straczynski, a television writer and producer who has taught scriptwriting for years, says it can be anyone. He's taught all kinds of people, including high school students, housewives, mechanics, and published authors.[1] Great scripts—both telescripts (scripts for TV shows) and movie screenplays—have been written by a wide variety of people. So you might decide to try your hand at it.

If you've written an entirely original script, then you have no copyright concerns. That's true even if you've based your movie on an event that actually happened, like the explosion of the space shuttle *Challenger* in 1986. But what if you've based your film on a short story you read? Or what if you've been inspired by someone else's movie? In both cases, you've written what lawyers would call a derivative work. Remember, a derivative work is one that is derived from, or based on, another. That's going to be a problem, but only in certain situations. A problem would arise if you are going to make money off your project. Are you planning eventually to show your film to an audience and charge them admission? It may also be a problem if you're going to post your film on a Web site.

What if you want to use someone else's script, either in its entirety or just in part? (Some scripts have been published and can be found in a bookstore or library.) Although using someone else's script for an amateur film may not require permission, you will certainly need to acknowledge that this is not your own work in the credits. Include the name of the author and the script.[2]

Sometimes young filmmakers want to use music in their works. Professional movie producers get permission to use art and recorded music in their films, and you should, too. It may be easier to get musicians to record music just for your movie.[3] (If you do so, you'll still need to get rights to use a copyrighted song or piece of music, but at least you would not have to get the permission—or pay the fees—to use someone else's recording.) Recently, some record companies have announced that they're not going to protest if their music is used in YouTube films, for example. They regard this as good advertising. The RIAA, however, is going after the makers of some YouTube films that use copyrighted music.[4]

Film companies also manage how they show everyday items in their films. They work out deals with companies to show their products, sometimes in the background or being used by the characters. This practice is called product placement. Carmakers, computer and software firms, and soda companies are just a few of the types of businesses that pay to have their products appear in movies, music videos, and video games. While this need not concern student filmmakers, it would still be wise to be careful what is shown in a movie. For example, using a brand-name product in a way that portrays it negatively may lead to some trouble with the product's manufacturer if the company finds out about it. For example, the company may hear about the film after it wins an award at a big-name film festival.

Students aren't usually held accountable for including footage that features a piece of copyrighted art in their films. The artwork could be a statue in a plaza where they're shooting, for example. The copyright expert William W. Fisher III questions whether this is all right. He concludes, however, "It is far from clear that such permissions are legally necessary."[5] More and more often, professional movie producers are also taking the time to get permissions from real-life people who happen to appear in their films, as well as permission to use footage of real estate.

Copyright and Film

How does copyright apply to film in the United States? When it comes to music, there are two types of copyrights: the song copyright and the recording copyright. With video and film, there are also two copyrights. The first covers the script. Today, that's automatically established as soon as the scriptwriter writes down his or her words. The second, the movie copyright, belongs to the production companies that make it. So it's Lucasfilm Ltd. that owns the movie copyright to *Star Wars,* not George Lucas himself. Under copyright law, it's the person or company who owns the script to a television show or a movie who decides how that script can be used. This means you cannot post part of a script on your Web site or blog without permission. Under the fair use doctrine, you can quote a few lines, but only in a review or criticism. You're not supposed to publish any part of the script. This means you can't even post your favorite lines from your favorite movie on your Web site without permission.

Copyright law also has a clause that says production companies can sue if someone rips off their ideas, making a "substantially similar" work.[6] They have the exclusive right to prepare derivative works, editing their film for TV, remaking it, or producing a sequel. Copyright law also restricts the use of characters. This is sometimes very broadly interpreted. For instance, a court ruled the carmaker Honda could not use an unnamed man who shared many traits with film superspy James Bond in a commercial.[7]

Production companies also have the right to public performance, meaning they get to decide where and when their works will be shown. Every time a movie is shown in a theater, on a pay-per-view channel, on a premium movie channel, or on an airplane, the copyright owner collects a fee. They also decide when they'll release a movie on video and to which countries and regions, as well as when a movie can be shown on TV. Once a DVD or video has been released, they don't have any control, however, over rentals, deciding who can rent it or for how long, for example. It's also the right of a movie's copyright owner to license movie-related merchandise. This means they get to decide who makes toys, T-shirts, and posters featuring their characters.

Copying Video

Students may occasionally want to use video in a school project. But many would like to be able to have their own private stash of favorite video clips that they could view on their computer whenever they liked. What's the deal, then? When are individuals allowed to copy video for their own personal use?

Usually it's a production company that owns the copyright to a movie or TV show. That means it has what lawyers call the exclusive right of reproduction. It gets to dictate how and when a movie can be copied and distributed. It even regulates how movie or TV show clips can be used.

Under what circumstances can you copy video? Think about these situations. You're a huge fan of the San Antonio Spurs. You can't be home to watch a game on TV. Is it fair for you to record it to play later? Yes. But you can't show that recording at a party or to a club at school. And you can never charge viewers money to watch the video.

Teachers are allowed to show a class films or TV shows for educational purposes but not for entertainment.[8] Teachers aren't even allowed to make a DVD of clips, because under the law, that's considered making a derivative work. For example, a history teacher wants to show the class how Mexican Americans have been portrayed in movies. He or she can't put together a collection of different movie scenes even to help illustrate the point he or she is trying to make. The teacher has to put one DVD in the player, select the relevant scene, show it, eject it, and then put in another to show the next scene. Teachers are also not supposed to cut out commercials, although they can use the remote control to fast-forward through them. What's more, they aren't supposed to record the video without the audio track (although they are allowed to mute the sound when they're playing the video).

You can record a movie on television for your personal use, but you can't post a clip from it on your Web site.

Now consider this situation. You are a big fan of Jim Carrey. You see that one of his earliest movies is playing on one of the cable channels. Is it fair for you to record it? Yes, you can record the video for your personal use. But it's against the law for you to post a clip on your Jim Carrey fan Web site.

Lately, the movie industry has made a huge effort to educate viewers about the dangers of piracy. It's fighting back against what's called bootlegging. Bootlegged movies are made when someone enters a movie theater and tapes a movie using a video camera. This is absolutely illegal to do, whether you're making a tape to view by yourself later or whether you intend to burn the movie onto a thousand DVDs and sell them. Today pirated DVDs—DVDs that have been copied illegally—are available for sale all over the world. American moviemakers are especially angry over the sales of millions of pirated DVDs in China and other Asian countries. The sale of these pirated DVDs causes them to lose millions of dollars.

What about an individual copying a DVD? There are DVD burners for sale. Your laptop or personal computer might have the capacity to burn a DVD. The courts have long held that a buyer has the right to make a copy of something for his or her own personal use. That's why you can photocopy a book that's falling apart or copy a CD to listen to in the car. But in the case of DVDs, the question is trickier. DVDs are generally electronically copy-protected so that it is physically impossible to make a copy. Courts have ruled that you cannot legally override that copy protection. You're not supposed to copy the DVD you purchased onto an MP3 player, handheld gaming device, PDA, or notebook computer.[9]

In the future, people who do not like this interpretation of the law hope you will be allowed to copy your DVD of *The Lord of the Rings: The Two Towers*, for example, for yourself. Would you be able to copy it for your friend? The answer is obvious—no. What about copying DVDs that are not copy-protected? You are allowed to copy DVDs that are in the public domain and your own home movies, for instance.[10]

How to Know if a Movie Is in the Public Domain

1. It may have documentation that says so.

2. Ask a librarian to help you find the address for a motion picture clearinghouse. Contact it to inquire about the film.

3. If the motion picture clearinghouse says it does not know, contact the United States Copyright Office.

One thing you are allowed to do is copy a movie from a videotape onto a blank DVD if it's not yet available for sale on a DVD. You can also do this with old TV shows you recorded.[11] What about movies you've recorded on a service like TiVo? You're not supposed to copy those onto a DVD.[12] Today a copyright owner can prevent a particular show from being recorded on a DVR or can use TiVo technology to cause it to be deleted automatically after a certain amount of time.

What is allowed in terms of foreign movies? Imagine that a friend of yours went to Japan on foreign study. She came back with a DVD of an anime show that fascinates you. It hasn't been shown on TV in the United States and isn't available on DVD. Can she copy it for you? That would be wrong. It's the same as copying a movie that was bought here.

In some cases, an individual might be tempted to copy a foreign movie that is not yet available here and sell it, maybe on eBay. That's wrong, too. In fact, it would be much more serious. What if someone copies it and sells thousands of copies in China? That's commonly referred to as piracy, and it's a very serious problem today. In fact, video piracy is such a problem that it's investigated by both the FBI and the Immigration and Customs Enforcement agency.

Downloading Videos

People like to download videos using the Internet in the same way they like to download music. Today, there are sites and services that offer legal downloads. But there are also plenty of sites that offer illegal downloads. To use these sites is to take a huge risk. Copyright owners are represented by groups like the RIAA and the Motion Picture Association of America (MPAA). These groups have sued some individuals over illegal download-ing. They've also launched advertising campaigns designed to educate viewers about who gets hurt when people illegally download or pirate a movie. News stories about downloading lawsuits and the advertising campaigns seem to be helping with the problem. In the past two years, illegal down-loading has decreased by 7 percent.[13] Nevertheless, it's still a problem. You must understand the impli-cations of illegal downloading. To use a service such as BitTorrent, eDonkey, or DirectConnect to share copyrighted movies or TV shows is strictly illegal.[14] This is theft. And the movie industry takes it very seriously. In November of 2005, the MPAA sued a grandfather after his grandson illegally downloaded four movies onto his grandfather's personal computer. The *Milwaukee Journal Sentinel* reported that the two sides settled the case. The grandfather agreed to pay a fine of $4,000.[15]

Downloading Software and Video Games

Software is a program that lets your computer perform a specific task. You probably use word processing software to write your research papers. A graphics package that lets you manipulate digital photos is also a type of software. And games you play on your computer, such as Oregon Trail or Civilization, are another form of software.

How does the concept of fair use apply to software? When you buy software, companies often want you to agree to certain terms, or conditions, of use. Sometimes you do this when you register your software. Sometimes you agree to do so just by opening the packaging. It's important to read the documentation. In almost all cases, you're allowed to make a back-up copy in case your machine goes down. You're also allowed to install software on two machines that you own. After all, some people use a desktop computer at home but have a laptop they take on trips. What you're not allowed to do, however, is allow someone else to download or copy your software. You can't e-mail a copy to someone else.[16] You also must not copy someone else's software, be it a friend's or your school's or from some other place. It's also important to be careful when you're buying software so that you don't get tricked into buying something that has been pirated. You also should not use peer-to-peer sharing programs to get software that someone else has copied illegally.

People often download software. In fact, many times when you buy software, you get it as a download. There's also software out there that is legally available for free. It's often called freeware. As the name suggests, freeware is software that costs nothing to obtain. Adobe® Reader® is an example of freeware. One very easy way to find freeware is to use that term as your search phrase and perform an Internet search. You can do the same to find shareware. The authors of shareware allow their programs to be downloaded for free. They ask users to pay a small fee only if they find the programs useful.[17]

Clearly, it's against the law to hack your way around password protection to let you access software, or to extend your use of a computer program to which your subscription has expired.[18] There are legal downloads out there of games by companies such as EA Games, but you will have to pay for them. They're easily located by doing an Internet search. But if you're strapped for cash, you will have to content yourself with the free games you can download through sites like Yahoo!

How to Identify Pirated Software

1. The price is extremely low.

2. It comes without a box.

3. If it has a box, the printing on it is not of high quality. Perhaps the colors don't look right or words are misspelled.

4. Its name isn't quite right. (For example, a television show once featured a phone called the Nokio, rather than the Nokia—rip-off artists use tricks like this on all kinds of pirated items.)

5. It's not shrink-wrapped.

6. And the primary sign—it's on a blank CD that has no printed label.

If you see software for sale on an auction site like eBay, take the time to read the description carefully. If it does not say that you will get a license agreement, manual, box, and certificate of authenticity, e-mail the seller to ask whether you will receive them. All of those will come with legal software.[19]

File sharing is when computer users in different locations make digital files available over the Internet. In peer-to-peer networks, users download and install software that lets them access a provider's server, through which they can search for and locate files on other people's computers and then obtain them. So it's technically incorrect to call it file sharing. After all, there's not one file that many people are sharing. Each person goes to get his or her own copy. (It's also wrong to call this file swapping—there's no trade involved.)

There's nothing wrong with the idea behind file sharing, but people have misused the application. According to Gretchen Hoffmann, the author of a book about copyrights, "To date, this technology has been used primarily to copy and exchange digital files of songs and movies without authorization of copyright owners."[20] It is the corporations and organizations who hold the copyrights to huge repertories of works that get most upset by file sharing—and do the most to try to prevent it and punish those who do it. The most aggressive work is done by the Recording Industry Association of America (RIAA).

There are legal and ethical reasons not to use illegal file-sharing services. But there are other more practical reasons, too. Often, using them causes you to download viruses onto your machine without your knowledge. According to *Wired News,* downloads from Kazaa very often carried malware, or a type of software designed to cause harm to your computer.[21] (The prefix *mal-* means "evil.") A security company also warns that some peer-to-peer programs make everything on your computer available to other users![22]

Chapter 9

Permissions

PERMISSION—IT'S ONE OF THOSE WORDS that have more than one meaning. Kids learn its basic definition at an early age. They ask their parents for permission to go to the movies or an instructor's permission to borrow a book. In these cases, they're simply asking to be allowed to do something.

But the word *permission* also has a more specific, legal meaning. When lawyers talk about a permission, they're referring to a formal, written document that gives consent, or allows, someone to use copyrighted material. Publishers ask for a permission when they want to reproduce the painting *The Scream* in a biography of the artist Edvard Munch. *Sports Illustrated* magazine asks for permission when it wants to use an official photo from the X Games to illustrate an article. If someone wants to download or scan the cover of the latest Black Eyed Peas CD to put up on a Web site, that's going to require permission, too.

When No Permission Is Necessary

There are situations under which U.S. law allows for the use or reproduction of someone else's material without permission. First, there is never a need for permission to use material that's in the public domain. Lawyers use that legal term to refer to works that are not copyrighted. In most cases, this means that the book, music, or other material was formerly copyrighted, but now the copyright has run out. (Copyrights are for a long, but limited, time. Lawyers say they "expire.") In fewer cases, the material was never copyrighted. The U.S. government intentionally does not copyright some material in order to make it available to anyone. Everything else that is written or created is automatically copyrighted. This was not true in the past, however. Before 1978, people had to register and then renew copyrights.

Second, the fair use of copyrighted material is permitted. Remember that it is legal to quote or reproduce another person's copyrighted work to comment on it or criticize it[1]—for a review or news story, for example. Imagine a student is reviewing the rapper Ludacris's new CD for a student newspaper. She can quote a few lines from his big hit song. But it is still important to provide the proper credit information—to say she's quoting and what her source is.

As discussed earlier, students, teachers, and scholars can draw from copyrighted materials for educational use under the fair use guidelines. So a student who's writing a paper or making a presentation doesn't need permission to quote from the latest biography of Eleanor Roosevelt or to include a political cartoon that made fun of her in a multimedia presentation. Teachers are allowed to use small parts of a work to educate students. And scholars are allowed to quote earlier works to build an argument. Look at Robert Caro's biography of President Lyndon Baines Johnson, for example. It includes many quotations and paraphrases from other sources. Caro footnoted the material he drew from, but he didn't have to get permission for every use.

When Is Permission Necessary?

Fair use means that students don't need to get permission to use copyrighted material when they're doing schoolwork. When they're writing a research paper or doing a class presentation, they do not need permission to quote a book, magazine article, poem, song, or speech. They are allowed to include in their work a photocopy that shows a photo of a CD cover.

There are, however, plenty of times when someone involved in an extracurricular activity, even one sponsored by a school, will need to get permission. For example, some students work for school newspapers. Perhaps the editor has seen a great article, political cartoon, or photograph in another publication. He can't just reprint it.

Copyright Term and the Public Domain in the United States

UNPUBLISHED WORKS

Type of Work	Copyright Term	What was in the public domain in the U.S. as of January 1, 2007
Unpublished works	Life of the author + 70 years	Works from authors who died before 1937
Unpublished anonymous and pseudonymous works, and works made for hire (corporate authorship)	120 years from date of creation	Works created before 1887
Unpublished works created before 1978 that were published after 1977 but before 2003	Life of the author + 70 years or December 31, 2047, whichever is greater	Nothing. The soonest the works can enter the public domain is January 1, 2048
Unpublished works created before 1978 that were published after December 31, 2002	Life of the author + 70 years	Works of authors who died before 1937
Unpublished works when the death date of the author is not known	120 years from date of creation	Works created before 1887

Copyright Term and the Public Domain in the United States

WORKS PUBLISHED IN THE UNITED STATES

Date of Publication	Conditions	Copyright Term
Before 1923	None	In the public domain
1923 through 1977	Published without a copyright notice	In the public domain
1978 to March 1, 1989	Published without notice, and without subsequent registration	In the public domain
1978 to March 1, 1989	Published without notice, but with subsequent registration	70 years after the death of author, or if work of corporate authorship, the shorter of 95 years from publication, or 120 years from creation
1923 through 1963	Published with notice but copyright was not renewed	In the public domain

Copyright Term and the Public Domain in the United States

WORKS PUBLISHED IN THE UNITED STATES

Date of Publication	Conditions	Copyright Term
1923 through 1963	Published with notice and the copyright was renewed	95 years after publication date
1964 through 1977	Published with notice	95 years after publication date
1978 to March 1, 1989	Published with notice	70 years after death of author, or if work of corporate authorship, the shorter of 95 years from publication, or 120 years from creation
After March 1, 1989	None	70 years after death of author, or if work of corporate authorship, the shorter of 95 years from publication, or 120 years from creation

Copyright Term and the Public Domain in the United States

WORKS PUBLISHED OUTSIDE THE UNITED STATES

Date of Publication	Conditions	Copyright Term in the United States
Before July 1, 1909	None	In the public domain
Works Published Abroad Before 1978 in Compliance with U.S. Formalities		
July 1, 1909, through 1922	Published in compliance with U.S. formalities	In the public domain
1923 through 1977	Published with notice, and still in copyright in its home country as of January 1, 1996	95 years after publication date
Works Published Abroad Before 1978 Without Compliance with U.S. Formalities		
July 1, 1909, through 1922	Published in a language other than English and without subsequent republication with a copyright notice	In the 9th Judicial Circuit, the same as for an unpublished work; in the rest of the U.S., likely to be in the public domain
1923 through 1977	In the public domain in its home country as of January 1, 1996	In the public domain

Copyright Term and the Public Domain in the United States

Works Published Abroad Before 1978 Without Compliance with U.S. Formalities

Date of Publication	Conditions	Copyright Term in the United States
1923 through 1977	Published in a language other than English, without subsequent republication with a copyright notice, and not in the public domain in its home country as of January 1, 1996	In the 9th Judicial Circuit, the same as for an unpublished work; in the rest of the U.S., likely to be 95 years after publication date
1923 through 1977	Published in English, without subsequent republication with a copyright notice, and not in the public domain in its home country as of January 1, 1996	95 years after publication date
Works Published Abroad After January 1, 1978		
After January 1, 1978	Copyright in the work in its home country has not expired by January 1, 1996	70 years after death of author, or if work of corporate authorship, the shorter of 95 years from publication, or 120 years from creation
Special Cases		
After July 1, 1909	Created by a resident of Afghanistan, Bhutan, Ethiopia, Iran, Iraq, Nepal, San Marino, and possibly Yemen, and published in one of these countries	Not protected by U.S. copyright law because they are not party to international copyright agreements

This chart was first published in Peter B. Hirtle, "Recent Changes To The Copyright Law: Copyright Term Extension," *Archival Outlook*, January/February 1999. This version is current as of January 1, 2007.

Permission is required in such cases. This also pertains to student yearbooks. Imagine there's a school club that has a Web site. Clearly the Webmaster can post on the site any material its members create. But she can't just copy material from another Web site.[2] A theater club can't download material from a Broadway show's Web site, for example, to repost it.

What about outside of school? The same rules apply to personal Web sites. A Johnny Depp fan may have a Web page devoted to him. It's against the law for that person to go to Disney's Web site and download a copy of a movie poster to put up on his or her own site. That same fan also can't quote more than a few words from *Newsweek*'s cover article about Johnny Depp. It's important to realize that it's strictly illegal to put up a chapter from a book on a Web page. Authors are very concerned today about what are called their electronic rights.[3]

Students also work on writing and art projects outside of school. Say a teenager is ready to write a novel. What he wants to do is tell the back story for the character named Jake, whom Stephen King created for his Dark Tower series. Wait. He can write what's termed fan fiction for his own personal satisfaction, but he'll need permission from King and his publisher if the story is going to appear in print. Fictional characters are protected by copyright law.[4]

The same applies to art, including comic book art. People all over the world draw manga characters, creating fan art. This is fine, unless they will somehow profit from it. They need to get permission before they put a poster of their drawing or painting up on eBay, for example.

These rules also affect budding entrepreneurs. Someone has a great idea for merchandise. Hold on—they can't use a licensed character or company logo on a T-shirt or coffee mug without permission. What's more, no one is allowed to use a celebrity's name, photograph, likeness, or voice as part of a commercial enterprise without his or her consent. That's not a matter of copyright. Americans have what's called the right of publicity, which allows them "to control the commercial use of his or her name, likeness, or identity."[5] So no one can photograph members of a sports team or firefighters and publish a calendar featuring them without their consent.

Searching for the Evidence

So even students find themselves in situations where they need permission. Most people do not realize it, but if they paid attention when reading a book or watching a movie, they'd see plenty of permissions statements. Read Stephen King's *On Writing,* for instance. In it, he quotes two songs—Donovan Leitch's "There Is a Mountain" and John Prine's "Granpa Was a Carpenter."

On the copyright page (which *usually* immediately follows the title page), there are his permission statements for those lyrics. A book about Hawaii will have credits for all its photos. They probably appear right under the photos. They also might appear in a credits list at the beginning or end of the book.

How about in a video production? When the television news programs include a clip from another program, they have to get permission and provide a credit. Likewise, the producers of a television show have to get permission to use footage from an old news program. If the people in a movie watch *The Simpsons* or *American Idol,* the movie producers have gotten permission to use that TV clip. Think about watching the Super Bowl or another big sports event. There is a message that comes on the screen warning viewers not to tape and show the game to the public. Sports organizations strongly protect their copyrights.

How about music? Just look at the liner notes that are printed in the booklet that comes with any CD. Musicians have to get permissions, too, to record songs they haven't written. Film producers likewise have to get permission to use a song in their movie.

Why Are Permissions Necessary?

Copyright laws protect the rights of a person or company that produces a creative work. The work can take a wide variety of forms. It can be a literary work (a book, a poem, a magazine article, and similar materials), a movie, a piece of music, a piece of art, a photograph, software, or an industrial design. Copyright owners have the right to decide how their work may be used and whether it can be copied. That's the bottom line. By granting permission, they have decided that the other person can use their work.

How to Get Permission

1. Decide whether you need permission. You don't if you're working on a project for a specific class. But if you're working on a student publication or a Web site or are creating something to sell, you will need to get permission to quote from a source unless you're writing a review or a parody. Still confused about permissions? A librarian will be able to show you many good books about copyrights and permissions. You can also find them on your own using the library catalog.

2. Find out who the copyright owner is for the work you want to copy or reproduce.

3. Find out how to contact the copyright owner or a representative who can grant permission.

4. Request permission.

5. Negotiate any payment.

6. Keep track of your permissions.

Finding a Copyright Owner

To figure out whether you need permission to use material, you should first think about the fair use doctrine. If your use would not be considered a fair use under the law, you need permission. What then?

The first step is figuring out who holds a copyright. This means you need to look for a formal copyright notice on whatever you want to quote or copy. This is often very easy to find for a hardcover book. The name of the publisher will be on the title page. The publisher's mailing address often appears on the copyright page. (You might also look for a Web site address. Many publishers' Web sites have information regarding permissions.) Things are a little trickier when you're dealing with a paperback. Many times paperbacks are published by a different company than the one that published the hardcover, which owns the copyright. (The paperback publisher has obtained the rights to publish its version of the book from the original publisher.) Again, check the copyright page. It will say who owns the original copyright. What if you can't find an address for the publisher? In that case, go to a library. Reference tools such as *Literary Market Place, International Literary Market Place,* and *Books in Print* have long lists of publishers.

But what if you want to reproduce or quote from material that appeared in a magazine? Most magazines have a masthead, or list, that says who

Sample Copyright Page from This Book

Copyright © 2008 Enslow Publishers, Inc. ◄——— **copyright holder**

All rights reserved.

No part of this book may be reproduced by any means without the written permission of the publisher.

Library of Congress Cataloging-in-Publication Data

Gaines, Ann.
    Don't steal copyrighted stuff! : avoiding plagiarism and illegal ◄——— **title and author name**
internet downloading / Ann Graham Gaines.
        p. cm.
    Summary: "Learn how to research and write reports with proper citations and bibliographies. Also find out how to protect your own creative works"—Provided by publisher.
    Includes bibliographical references and index.
    ISBN-13: 978-0-7660-2861-6 (alk. paper)
    ISBN-10: 0-7660-2861-5 (alk. paper)
    1. Plagiarism. 2. Bibliographical citations. 3. Downloading of data. ◄——— **subject headings**
    4. Copyright infringement. I. Title.
    PN167.G35 2008
    808—dc22
                                2007008370

Printed in the United States of America

10 9 8 7 6 5 4 3 2 1

To Our Readers:
We have done our best to make sure that all Internet Addresses in this book were active and appropriate when we went to press. However, the author and publisher have no control over and assume no liability for the material available on those Internet sites or on other Web sites they may link to. Any comments or suggestions can be sent by e-mail to comments@enslow.com or to the address on the back cover.

Cover Photo: © Comstock/Corbis. **Interior Photos:** Acclaim Images/Verna Bice, ◄——— **photo credits**
p. 49; Acclaim Images/Felipe Rodriguez, p. 69; Acclaim Images/Mary-Ella Keith, p. 109; Alamy/Visual Arts Library (London), p. 96; Associated Press, p. 31; AP/Chitose Suzuki, p.5; AP/John S. Stewart, p.174; AP/Cheryl Gerber, p.12; AP/Rich Pedroncelli, p. 167; AP/Bruce Lee, p. 131; AP/Greg Swiercz, p.103; AP/Paul Sakuma, p. 123; Christine Balderas, pp. 71, 74, 76; Getty Images/Joe Raedle, p. 8; Getty Images/Robert Sullivan, p.44; iStockphoto.com/Dovile Butvilaite, pp. 72, 73, 74, 164; iStockphoto.com/Rarpia, p. 2, 159.

publishes a magazine and gives their address. It usually appears near the front of the magazine. If you're having trouble, consult a librarian. In some cases, a magazine might have purchased only certain rights to a story or article. In that case, you might have to contact the author. You might look on the Web for an address or phone number. But you might also need to contact the Authors Registry or the Publication Rights Clearinghouse.

What if you want to quote from a newspaper? Many newspapers put at least some of their contact information online. Go to *The New York Times* Web site, for example, to find information about how to contact them to get permission.[6]

To use a photograph that you've seen in a book, magazine, or newspaper, you will most likely need to contact the photographer. How are you going to find out who that is? Check the caption. In the case of a book, you might also want to look at the photo credits list. Many photographers can be found by doing a Web search. An alternative is to contact the publisher who used the photo. Copyright does apply to new art, but it no longer applies to many older works of fine art. Nevertheless, if you've seen a photograph of that work of art, there's another copyright involved—that held by the museum that owns the work or the person who took the photograph. So for a work of art, it's best to check the captions or credit list in the source where you saw its photograph. You can find contact information for many artists and museums on the Web. Be warned—if the piece you're interested in is owned by a private collector, it might be very hard to get permission to reproduce it.

To record someone else's song as well as reprint song lyrics (its words) or music, you must contact the music publisher. How can you do this? If you own a CD with the music you want to use, look at its liner notes. If you want to quote lyrics, you'll need the name of the music publisher. If you want to perform a song or play a CD in a public setting (that means on the radio or even at a club or restaurant), you'll need the name of the recording company and the name of the music publisher (you're going to need what's called a double permission).[7] The Music Publishers' Association is a good group to ask for information as to how to contact a music publisher. To find out how to contact a recording company, you might start by contacting the Recording Industry Association of America.

What if you want to reproduce a photograph that records a scene from a movie or TV program? This requires permission from the production company. That name will appear on the screen at the beginning or end of the show. You can also find contact information for production companies by searching the Internet.

And last, but certainly not least, what if you want to use material you find on the Internet? This is one area where copyright owners are becoming more and more aggressive, seeking to protect their content. Look at the bottom of a Web page. Most have a link that will connect you to a site's administrator.

In any of these cases, if you have trouble figuring out whom to contact, one good thing to do is to ask a librarian at your school or public library for help.

Requesting Permission

So you know that you need permission and you've figured out the company or organization to contact. First, check its Web page to see if there's a Web form to fill out. If there's not, you might want to call the company to ask whether to send an e-mail or a fax. It's always all right to send a letter. One problem is knowing who, specifically, to address it to. Perhaps you will be able to get the name of an individual to contact by doing a Web search or by calling the company that holds the copyright. But in most cases, you'll be all right just addressing a letter to the permissions department.

Whatever form your request takes, it should have some specific things. You will need to say exactly what it is you want to use. In the case of a book, you will need to include the author's name, the title of the book, and the year it was copyrighted. It is very helpful to send a photocopy of the passage you want to quote. You will need to send similar information regarding art (the name of the artist, the title of the piece, and the book or

Web site where you saw it). For music, you'll also need to know the name of the musician and the piece of music you want to use.

You will need to state your purpose or describe your project. Give your name and the title of your project. Describe your project. What is it you're going to produce? The copyright holder is going to want to know which magazine is going to publish your fan fiction, for example. If you want Web rights—if you're asking for permission to put something up on your Web site—the copyright holder will want to know your site's URL and how long you want to keep it up. They will especially want to know whether there will be money made from this use. If you want permission to use a play, for example, it's best to note how many performances will be given, how many people you expect to buy tickets, and how much will be charged per ticket.

If you're sending a letter or a fax, make a place for an authorized company representative or an artist to sign at the bottom. When you send off the letter, be sure to include more than one copy— one for the owner of the copyright to retain and one to be sent back to you. If you're sending an e-mail, he or she will be able to grant you permission simply by replying to yours.

What If You Don't Get Permission?

In some cases, people realize they have failed to get the permission they need. This can be very scary.

Sample Permissions Letter

[Your name]
[Your address]

[The date]

[The name of the person you're writing to]
[His or her address]

Dear _____,

    Please permit me to introduce myself. I am a student working on a [describe your project here, in detail, explaining how many copies of your student magazine are printed and how much they'll be sold for]. I would like your permission to use in my project excerpts from [the creator's name and title of what you want permission to reproduce]. I want to reproduce [describe the text. You should also include a photocopy of the material you want to use.]

    Granting me these rights will in no way restrict republication of the material in any other form by you or by others authorized by you. Your signing of this letter will also confirm that you own the copyright to the above-described material.

    If these arrangements meet with your approval, please sign this letter where indicated below and return it to me in the enclosed return envelope. Thank you very much.

Sincerely,
[Your name and signature]

PERMISSION GRANTED FOR THE USE REQUESTED
ABOVE: ___[Signature line for addressee]_____
[Type name of addressee below signature line]
Date: _____

Perhaps you've published your zine without getting permission to use a comic strip. You still need to seek the permission. You may have to pay a penalty. Know that in some extreme cases, people have had to pull a product out of circulation because of copyright problems.

If you infringe on a copyright holder's legal rights, you may find yourself in serious legal trouble. Courts hear many copyright infringement cases. Sometimes, of course, they rule on the side of the accused. But there have been many other cases in which a judge rules that there has been copyright infringement. American courts can assess fines of $250 to $150,000 for a single copyright infringement. If you copy a work (pirate a CD or DVD, in other words), you could receive a jail sentence of five years and have to pay a huge fine![8]

Tracking Permissions

Perhaps the nature of your project means you're going to need only one permission. In some cases, though, you'll need more than one. Whatever the case, one very important thing to do is keep track of your permissions. Keep them in a special file or folder. Don't forget to make a note to yourself if you're granted permission to use an image, say, on a Web site for just a limited time. You'll have to remember either to take it down or to write to ask for an extension at the right time.

Chapter 10

How to Protect
Your Own Rights

IT'S IMPORTANT FOR STUDENTS to avoid violating other people's rights. But there are also many situations in which they will want to prevent other people from infringing on their rights. After all, writers and other creative people work hard, and it would not be fair if they did not get the credit they deserve. Think about a person who found out that someone else was set to make $1 million off the comic book character he or she created. He or she would be extremely angry. That might be far-fetched. What happens more frequently is that people post other people's photographs, for example, on the Internet. There are also those cases where one student steals another student's paper.

Keep Your Schoolwork Safe

You know that you should not cheat. But did you know that it's also your responsibility to keep other

You can help friends with an assignment by discussing it with them—but don't give them your own work to copy.

people from cheating from you? This means that you must keep your work to yourself. It's all right to talk about assignments with other students in your class. You should not show work you're doing to other people, however. This applies not just to research papers but to programming code you're writing for a computer science class or to the findings you obtained in a chemistry lab, for example. If your teacher is grading papers and sees very similar work being turned in by several students, he or she will find it very difficult to figure out who is copying from whom. Everyone involved will be in trouble.

As you know, educators believe plagiarism is a massive problem today. As a result, they're always on the lookout for plagiarized work.[1] Just in case you're ever falsely accused of plagiarism, it's a good idea to keep the materials you've used to put your assignment together. In the case of a research paper, keep your outline, your note cards, and your rough draft. That way, if your paper is stolen, you'll be able to prove that you were the one who actually wrote it.[2]

Do not loan out an old paper.

In some cases, you'll write a paper or do a project that you're especially proud of. You want to keep it. This is a great idea. Looking back over your work later will give you a great sense of self-confidence. Plus, one day, you might want access to the information you found for your paper or presentation. But beware. Do not loan out an old paper. People may ask to borrow one. Maybe it's for an honest reason. But you do not want to find out that your friend has ripped you off. Think of what might happen to your friendship—and your reputation. An instructor might think you encouraged the person to cheat. There are other ways to help a friend who's having trouble in a class. Offer to discuss ideas, recommend research resources, or suggest that he or she visit the school librarian or writing lab.

If you ever discover that someone is plagiarizing, you will have a hard decision to make. We live in an age when many people think there is nothing worse than "ratting out" someone else. But in many people's opinion, you must not look away. If your fellow student has yet to turn the work in, you can start by just talking to him or her. If he or she has already submitted the work, you could talk to the teacher or a school counselor. He or she will be able to handle the situation.[3]

Outside of Class

Maybe it seems like students don't need the protection offered by copyright law. This is not true. Lots of people who have yet to graduate from high school or college are already creating great work outside as well as inside the classroom. Literary magazines for teenagers such as *Cricket* and *Click* regularly invite their readers to send in short stories, poems, or artwork for contests. Students submit jokes, poems, short stories, comics, fan fiction, and lots of other kinds of writing to Web sites. They perform their poetry at slams all across the country. Some are lucky enough to have their paintings, prints, photographs, or sculptures

One important thing to realize is that there are things copyright does not protect. Under U.S. law, creators cannot copyright an idea or theory. They can only protect the way the idea or theory is expressed. While you will not be infringing on a copyright if you use someone else's idea, it would still be considered plagiarism if you did not give the person credit. When using the ideas or theories of others, you must credit your sources.

Also, other people have the right to use facts others have collected, even if it was very difficult to find them. For example, when researchers conduct a survey, they cannot limit how the information is used. Others can cite their findings in newspaper articles or on a Web site, but they must credit the source of the information.

Likewise, the law does not allow people to copyright a procedure or recipe—even if it's your aunt's very special cake. (Companies like Kentucky Fried Chicken can trademark their recipes and keep them secret.) You would secure a copyright, however, if you wrote a long account of how to bake a particular cake, making unusual word choices and adding descriptive phrases. It's the words, however, that you have rights to and not the manner in which the cake is made.[4] U.S. copyright law also says copyright cannot be applied to a title, name, short phrase, or slogan. For these things, people apply for trademarks. There are, however, a different set of laws that pertain to trademarks. That means companies can control the use of a title or name that's associated with a product. So you can't call your movie *Star Wars*.

displayed at a gallery or on the Internet. There are student songwriters, playwrights, and screenwriters. It's not just professionals—people who make money from their talent—who need to be able to protect their own work. Everybody has the right to protect their own work, no matter who they are.

All of these people need to think about how to go about protecting their work to prevent other people from copying it. What many people do not realize is that today, writers and other creators need to do absolutely nothing to secure a copyright for their work. Today's U.S. copyright law is clear. You secure copyright as soon as you "fix" or finish your creation. That means writing down your words or recording your music, either on sheet music or on a tape or CD.[5] Note that you do not have to publish your writing or record your music in a professional recording studio.

Securing a copyright is easy; it usually happens automatically when a work is created. But in many cases, that will not be enough if you have to go to court about copyright infringement. To do this, you must register your copyright. Say you discover that someone else is using your copyrighted material and you want to sue him or her. A U.S. work must be registered before an infringement lawsuit is brought. Registration of a copyright is fairly straightforward. It requires filling out a simple form, paying a fee of around $45, and depositing one or two copies of your work with the

United States Copyright Office. The best way to find out which form in particular you need to fill out is to go online to the copyright office's Web site.[6]

How to Register Your Copyright

Step 1: Create your work.

Step 2: Obtain the right form from the United States Copyright Office. (They're available online, along with instructions for completing them.)

Step 3: Fill out the form and return it, along with the required fee and the copy of your work you are depositing.

Step 4: Receive your copyright registration certificate.

Step 5: Place your certificate in a safe place.

If you have secured a copyright, no one is supposed to use or reproduce your material without your permission. If you've written a poem and put it up on your blog, for example, no one is allowed to download it and put it up on theirs without asking you first. In fact, if you realize that someone has downloaded some of your writing or a photo to put it up on his or her Web site, you have the right to demand that he or she remove it. You can do this through a cease-and-desist letter. To write one, you can find samples on the Internet or you can ask a librarian to help you find a book with an example of one. Having written a letter, you have not done enough to take legal action against the person who is ripping you off. You cannot take the person to court or demand damages (to collect money from them, in other words) without having registered your copyright.

How to Protect Your Web Site

Today, millions of individuals and organizations put up their own Web sites. Unfortunately, in many cases, their content is stolen. Web site authors find it very aggravating to see content they've slaved over appearing on someone else's Web site.

Protect your Web site by adding a copyright notice.

What can you do to protect your Web site? There are several steps you can take. First, make sure that you yourself created everything on your Web site. Post your permissions for any material you got from another source. Then post what is called a copyright notice on your Web site.[7] That can be just a line saying the work is copyrighted by [fill in the blank with your name] and the year you wrote or created your material. A sample copyright line might look like this: © 2008 by Bob Smith.

You can find sample cease-and-desist letters by doing a search on the Internet.

Think about adding a line of text that says that if people want to use your work, they should contact you. If anyone does so, you can think about whether to grant him or her permission. If the person is going to credit you and show your work in a positive light, you probably will. The next step is to write the person a formal letter of permission. To protect artwork and photos, in particular, you could buy software that will let you identify your artwork with a special symbol called a watermark.

How do you find out if someone is copying you? In some cases, a user will notify you. You can then follow up. You could do your own search, pasting in a big section of your text as your search term. You could use Google images search to see if any of your artwork or photos are being used.

What can you do if you discover someone is stealing your stuff? The first step is to write a cease-and-desist letter. You will need to send this both to the person who has put up the Web site that features your work and to the server that hosts his or her Web site. Give the person a short amount of time (perhaps two weeks) to change the site. If he or she does not, you might want to get advice from a lawyer.[8]

Protecting Your Work, Respecting Others' Work

Now you know how to protect your own work. Perhaps thinking about preventing other people from stealing your creative work has made you realize how important it is to respect the works of others. In school and out, it's absolutely essential to guard against plagiarism and illegal download-ing. To commit these acts is to harm yourself and others. To be caught will almost certainly cause you embarrassment and perhaps much more serious harm. It will remain important for you to guard against plagiarism and illegal downloading throughout your life. It's important for people of all ages and walks of life to understand how impor-tant it is not to take credit for other people's efforts or use copyrighted material without permission.

In the News

1. James Poniewozik and Andrea Sachs, "An F for Originality," *Time Canada,* May 8, 2006, p. 106.

2. David Zhou, "Student's Novel Faces Plagiarism Controversy," *The Harvard Crimson,* April 23, 2006, < http://www .thecrimson.com/article.aspx?ref=512948 > (August 13, 2006).

3. Rich Copley, "Young author's mistakes at heart of an author's fear," *Lexington Herald-Leader,* May 7, 2006, < http://www .kentucky.com/mld/kentucky/entertainment/columnists/ 14505661.htm > (August 13, 2006).

4. Poniewozik and Sachs, p. 106.

5. David R. Sands, "Researchers peg Putin as a plagiarist over thesis," *Washington Times,* March 25, 2006, p. A1.

6. Leslie Wayne, "Chief's Pay Is Docked by Raytheon," *The New York Times,* May 4, 2006, p. C1.

7. [Duke University] Center for Academic Integrity, "CAI Research," *Center for Academic Integrity* [Web site], 2007, < http://www.academicintegrity.org/cai_research.asp > (February 6, 2007).

Chapter 1 What Is Plagiarism?

1. San Diego Union High School, "Academic Honesty Policy," n.d., < http://sduhsd.k12.ca.us/district/instructionalservices/ academic_honesty/sduhsdacademic_honesty_ policy.htm > (August 15, 2006).

2. The University of Victoria [British Columbia], "Terms Used in the Calendar," 2005, < http://web.uvic.ca/calendar2005/ CAL/TUintC.html > (August 8, 2006).

3. Drew University, "Plagiarism—and how to avoid it!," n.d., < http://www.depts.drew.edu/composition/Avoiding_ Plagiarism.htm > (August 8, 2006).

4. Indiana University Bloomington Campus Writing Program, "Discouraging Plagiarism," updated August 2, 2006, < http://www.indiana.edu/ ~ cwp/plagiarism.shtml > (August 6, 2006).

5. Victoria University of Wellington, "Glossary," updated June 29, 2006, < http://www.vuw.ac.nz/home/glossary/ > (August 8, 2006).

6. Gananda School Library, "Plagiarism Is No Big Deal—Is It?," updated September 24, 2003, < http://www.gananda.org/ library/mshslibrary/plagexamples.htm > (August 9, 2006).

7. "Nothing New Under the Sun," *New Dictionary of Cultural Literacy,* revised edition (New York: Houghton Mifflin, 2002), p. 19.

8. Richard A. Polsner, "On Plagiarism," *Atlantic Monthly,* April 2002, p. 23.

9. OWL Program and Karl Stolley, "Avoiding Plagiarism," *Purdue University,* updated May 12, 2006, < http://owl.english .purdue.edu/owl/resource/589/01/ > (August 9, 2006).

10. David Callahan, *The Cheating Culture: Why More Americans Are Doing Wrong to Get Ahead* (Orlando, FL: Harcourt, 2004), pp. 199–205, 217–219.

11. John R. Endlund, "What Is 'Plagiarism' and Why Do People Do It?" *Cal State LA University Writing Center,* n.d., < http://www .calstatela.edu/centers/write_cn/plagiarism.htm > (February 8, 2007).

12. Robert A. Harris, "Anti-Plagiarism Strategies for Research Papers," *Virtual Salt,* November 17, 2004, < http://www .virtualsalt.com/antiplag.htm > (February 12, 2007).

13. "Statistics," *Plagiarism.org,* c. 1998–2001, < http://www .plagiarism.org/problem4.html > (August 15, 2006).

14. Center for Academic Integrity, "CAI Research," 2006, < http:// www.academicintegrity.org/cai_research.asp > (August 15, 2006).

Chapter 2 Types of Plagiarism

1. "W. T. Woodson Honor Code," 2004–2005, < http://www .fcps.edu/woodsonhs/guidance/academics/ai_honorcode .htm > (August 14, 2006).

2. Illinois Math and Science Academy, "Student/Parent Handbook," c. 1993–2006, < http://www.imsa.edu/living/ handbook/handbook.php#achonesty > (August 14, 2006).

3. Choate Rosemary Hall, "Honor Code," n.d., < http://www .choate.edu/summerprograms/student_community standards.asp > (August 14, 2006).

4. Margaret Fain and Peggy Bates, "Cheating 101: Paper Mills and You," revised January 25, 2005, < http://www.coastal .edu/library/presentations/papermil.html > (August 10, 2006).

5. University of Connecticut, "Anti-Plagiarism Strategies for Faculty," < www.lib.uconn.edu/campuses/stamford/using/ instruction/english/FacultyPresentation.ppt > (August 10, 2006).

6. "How Turnitin Plagiarism Prevention Works," n.d., <http://www.turnitin.com/static/resource_files/tii_process.pdf> (August 15, 2006).

7. Irving Hexham, "Academic Plagiarism Defined," c. 2005, <http://www.ucalgary.ca/~hexham/study/plag.html> (August 10, 2006).

8. Alexander Lindey, *Plagiarism and Originality.* (New York: Harper, 1952), p. 2.

9. Tom Lucey, "Dealing with Dishonesty," *Teachers.Net Gazette,* August 2002, <http://www.teachers.net/gazette/AUG02/lucey.html> (August 15, 2006).

10. Indiana University Bloomington Campus Tutorial Services, "Plagiarism: What It Is and How to Recognize and Avoid It," 2004, <http://www.indiana.edu/~wts/pamphlets/plagiarism.shtml> (February 12, 2007).

11. Melissa Walker, *Writing Research Papers: A Norton Guide* (New York: W. W. Norton, 1984), p. 73.

12. Dr. Miguel Roig, "Plagiarism and common knowledge," *Avoiding Plagiarism, Self-Plagiarism and Other Questionable Writing Practices: A Guide to Ethical Writing,* n.d., <http://facpub.stjohns.edu/~roigm/plagiarism/Plagiarism%20and%20common.html> (August 10, 2006).

13. Dwight Gardner, "Beg, borrow or. . . ." *Salon* (July 22, 1996), <http://www.salon.com/weekly/plagiarism960722.html> (August 10, 2006); [Syllabus, ENGL 1020, Regents Online Degree Program], n.d., <http://www.rodp.org/courses/syllabi/engl1020.htm> (August 10, 2006).

14. "Fan-fic," <http://www.answers.com/topic/fanfic#after_ad1>, (August 10, 2006); "Fanfic," <http://www.wordspy.com/words/fanfic.asp> (August 10, 2006).

15. "Fan fiction plagiarism," January 18, 2006, <http://www.plagiarismtoday.com/?p=161> (August 10, 2006).

16. Mark Lewis, "Doris Kearns Goodwin and the Credibility Gap," *Forbes,* February 27, 2002, <http://www.forbes.com/2002/02/27/0227goodwin.html> (February 8, 2007)

17. Seth Mnookin, "A Journalist's Hard Fall," *Newsweek,* May 19, 2003, reproduced in Peloso, p. 73.

18. "2005 Plagiarism Round-Up," *Regret the Error,* December 12, 2005, <http://www.regrettheerror.com/2005/12/2005_plagiarism.html> (August 10, 2006); "Famous Plagiarists Index," <http://www.famousplagiarists.com/indexnames.htm> (August 10, 2006).

Chapter 3 Understanding Copyright and Fair Use

1. Association of Research Libraries, "Timeline: A History of Copyright in the United States," modified November 22, 2002, <http://www.arl.org/info/frn/copy/timeline.html> (August 9, 2006).

2. U.S. Copyright Office, "Copyright Law of the United States," n.d., <http://www.copyright.gov/title17/> (August 9, 2006).

3. Lloyd J. Jassin and Steven C. Schechter, *The Copyright Permission and Libel Handbook: A Step-by-Step Guide for Writers, Editors, and Publishers* (New York: John Wiley & Sons, 1998), p. 26.

4. Ellen M. Kozak, *Every Writer's Guide to Copyright and Publishing Law* (New York: Henry Holt and Company, 1996), p. 42.

5. William W. Fisher III, *Promises to Keep: Technology, Law, and the Future of Entertainment* (Stanford, CA: Stanford Law and Politics, 2004), p. 44.

6. Library of Congress, Copyright Office, "Fair Use," Circular FL-102, June 1999, reproduced in Jennifer Peloso, editor, *Intellectual Property* (n.p.: H. W. Wilson, 2003), p. 22.

7. Tomas A. Lipinski, *The Complete Copyright Liability Handbook for Librarians and Educators* (New York: Neal-Schuman Publishers, 2006), p. 170.

8. About, Inc., "Copyright on the Web," 2006, <http://webdesign.about.com/od/copyright/a/aa081700a.htm> (July 24, 2006).

9. Gretchen McCord Hoffmann, *Copyright in Cyberspace 2: Questions and Answers for Librarians* (New York: Neal-Schuman, 2005), p. 62.

Chapter 4 Finding Sources and Taking Good Notes

1. Jack Lynch, "Guide to Grammar and Style," revised June 30, 2006, <http://andromeda.rutgers.edu/~jlynch/Writing/> (August 15, 2006).

2. Michigan State University Libraries, "Basic Citation Guides," revised July 27, 2006, <http://www.lib.msu.edu/harris23/general/citation.htm> (August 10, 2006).

3. Duke University, Online Writing Lab "Writing a Research Paper," c. 1995–2004, <http://owl.english.purdue.edu/workshops/hypertext/ResearchW/types.html> (February 6, 2007).

4. Melissa Walker, *Writing Research Papers: A Norton Guide* (New York: W. W. Norton, 1994), p. 4.

5. Emmy Misser, "The Research Paper [a Wilfrid Laurier University Writing Centre Handout]" n.d., < http://info.wlu.ca/writing/handouts/research.htm > (August 10, 2006).

6. Vaughan Memorial Library, Acadia University, "Plagiarism at Acadia: A Student's Guide," revised April 2005, < http://library.acadiau.ca/guides/plagiarism/student/index.html > (August 10, 2006).

7. The Learning Centre, University of New South Wales, "How does plagiarism happen? Poor time management," n.d., < http://www.lc.unsw.edu.au/plagiarism/how_2.html > (August 10, 2006).

8. Joseph Gibaldi, *MLA Handbook for Writers of Research Papers,* 6th edition (New York: The Modern Language Association of America, 2003), p. 11–14.

9. Jeffrey Strausser, *Painless Writing* (Hauppauge, New York: Barron's Educational Series, Inc., 2001), p. 35.

10. Walker, p. 11.

11. *How to Write Research Papers,* 3rd edition (Lawrenceville, New Jersey: Arco, 2002), pp. 18–20.

12. Aaron, Jane E., *The Little, Brown Essential Handbook for Writers,* 4th edition (N.p.: Addison-Wesley Educational Publishers, 2003), pp. 138–140; and Gibaldi, pp. 41–45.]

13. Education World, "Student Guide to Avoiding Plagiarism," *Education World,* c. 2002, < http://www.educationworld.com/a_curr/TM/curr390_guide.shtml > (August 10, 2006).

14. "NoodleTools," < http://www.noodletools.com/ > (August 10, 2006).

15. Walker, p. 71.

16. Walker, p. 73, Purdue University OWL, "Quotation marks," c. 1995–2004, < http://owl.english.purdue.edu/handouts/grammar/g_quote.html > (August 10, 2006).

17. "Paraphrase," n.d. < http://wordnet.princeton.edu/perl/webwn?s = paraphrase >, (August 10, 2006); Purdue University OWL, "Quoting, Paraphrasing and Summarzing," c. 1995–2004, < http://owl.english.purdue.edu/handouts/research/r_quotprsum.html > (August 10, 2006).

18. *How to Write Research Papers,* p. 27.

19. "Student Guide to Avoiding Plagiarism," *Education World,* c. 2002, < http://www.educationworld.com/a_curr/TM/curr390_guide.shtml > (August 10, 2006).

Chapter 5 Putting Together Your Project
Using Proper Citations

1. Thomas Saylor, "Creating an Effective PowerPoint Presentation," c. 2001–2005, < http://people.csp.edu/saylor/effective_powerpoint.htm > (August 10, 2006).

2. NPR, "Cut and Paste Plagiarism," February 14, 2006, < http://www.npr.org/templates/story/story.php?storyId = 5205929 > (August 10, 2006).

3. Niko Silvester, "Before You Turn It In," *Writing,* v. 27, #3 (November/December 2004), p. 22

4. Capital Community College Library, "Preparing and Using Outlines," < http://wwwold.ccc.commnet.edu/mla/outlines.shtml > (August 10, 2006).

5. "Student Guide to Avoiding Plagiarism," *Education World,* c. 2002, < http://www.educationworld.com/a_curr/TM/curr390_guide.shtml > (August 10, 2006).

6. Seattle Public Schools, "What Is Plagiarism?," < http://www.seattleschools.org/schools/meany/content/mmslibweb/htmlfiles/plagiarism.ppt > (August 10, 2006).

7. "Student Guide to Avoiding Plagiarism," *Education World,* c. 2002, < http://www.educationworld.com/a_curr/TM/curr390_guide.shtml > (August 10, 2006).

8. Boston College, English Department, First-Year Writing Program, "Guidelines for Dealing with Plagiarism in FWS," n.d., < http://monticello.bc.edu/fws/plagiarism > (August 10, 2006).

9. SUNY Geneseo Milne Library, "Plagiarism: Frequently Asked Questions," n.d., < http://library.geneseo.edu/research/plagiarismfaq.shtml > (August 14, 2006).

10. "Student Guide to Avoiding Plagiarism," *Education World,* c. 2002, < http://www.educationworld.com/a_curr/TM/curr390_guide.shtml > (August 10, 2006).

11. University of Victoria, "UVic Writer's Guide," c. 1995, < http://web.uvic.ca/wguide/Pages/CitPlagiarism.html > (August 10, 2006).

12. North Carolina State University Philosophy 375, "How to Use Verbatim Quotes," spring 2005, < http://social.chass.ncsu.edu/~kmmcshan/375/375HandoutVerbatim.htm > (August 10, 2006).

13. Purdue University Owl, "Quoting, Paraphrasing and Summarizing," c. 1995–2004, < http://owl.english.purdue.edu/handouts/research/r_quotprsum.html > (August 10, 2006).

Chapter Notes

14. Libraries, University of Iowa, "Strategies for Deterring Plagiarism," updated March 20, 2006), < http://www.lib .iastate.edu/commons/resources/facultyguides/plagiarism/ deter.html > (August 10, 2006).

Chapter 6 The Fair Use of Illustrations and Photos

1. Richard Stim, *Getting Permission: How to License and Clear Copyrighted Materials Online and Off* 2nd edition (Berkeley, CA: Nolo 2004), pp. 4/3 and 8/4.

2. Caroline Virr, "Fake That: Or How One Frustrated Artist and a Tin of Dulux Household Emulsion Fooled the Art World," *The Express* [Scottish Edition], May 6, 2006, p. 61.

3. "Debate Continues Over Intellectual-Property Boundaries," *The Philadelphia Inquirer,* October 15, 2003, p. NA. Accessed through InfoTrac OneFile, Gale Group Databases (July 7, 2006).

4. Timothy Egan, "Glass Artists Face Off in Court," *The New York Times,* June 1, 2006), p. A1.

5. Stim, p. 11/11.

Chapter 7 The Fair Use of Music and Sound

1. Richard Stim, *Getting Permission: How to License and Clear Copyrighted Materials Online and Off* 2nd edition (Berkeley, CA: Nolo 2004), p. 5/3.

2. "My Sweet Lord—George Harrison," *BBC Sold on Song Library,* n.d. < http://www.bbc.co.uk/radio2/soldonsong/ songlibrary/mysweetlord.shtml > (August 7, 2006).

3. William W. Fisher III, *Promises to Keep: Technology, Law, and the Future of Entertainment* (Stanford, CA: Stanford Law and Politics, 2004), p. 39.

4. Rebecca P. Butler, *Copyright for Teachers and Librarians* (New York: Neal-Schuman Publishers, 2004), p. 147.

5. "Music and Copyright," *Washington State University Publishing,* < http://publishing.wsu.edu/copyright/music_ copyright/ > (February 12, 2007).

6. Associated Press, "In Mexico, Internet Music Piracy Rising," *MSNBC.com,* July 1, 2006, < http://www.msnbc.msn.com/id/ 13617633/ > (February 12, 2007).

7. "CD Piracy in China," October 2003, < http://www.cluas.com/ music/features/piracy_china.htm > (August 7, 2006).

8. Jonathan Lamy et al., "RIAA Identifies 12 Piracy 'Hot-Spot' Cities," May 3, 2006, < http://www.riaa.com/News/ newsletter/050306.asp > (August 7, 2006).

9. Ibid.

10. "Napster launches legal downloads," May 20, 2004, < http://news.bbc.co.uk/cbbcnews/hi/music/newsid_3733000/3733357.stm > (August 7, 2006).

11. "Kazaa Settles RIAA Lawsuit," July 27, 2006, < http://www.plagiarismtoday.com/?p = 294 > (August 7, 2006).

12. "Apple Launches the iTunes Music Store," April 28, 2003, < http://www.apple.com/pr/library/2003/apr/28musicstore.html > (August 7, 2006).

13. Scott Thompson, "Studies show drop in illegal downloading," *Daily Universe,* via U-Wire, April 25, 2006.

14. David Bauder, "Memo to music industry: US fans say cut your prices, make better music," *Associated Press,* February 2, 2006, accessed through LexisNexis Academic database (July 31, 2006).

15. "Legal music downloading leaps in 2005," *CBC News,* July 13, 2005, < http://www.cbc.ca/arts/story/2005/07/13/DownloadsUp_050613.html (May 27, 2007).

16. "Eminem Sues Apple, MTC over iTunes Ad," *CNN.com,* February 24, 2004, < http://www.cnn.com/2004/TECH/internet/02/24/eminem.applesuit.ap/index > (February 12, 2007).

17. Stim, p. 5/9.

18. Creative Commons—Audio, n.d., < http://creativecommons.org/audio/ > (August 7, 2006).

19. Marshall Brain, "How Music Licensing Works: The Tale of Happy Birthday to You," < http://entertainment.howstuffworks.com/music-licensing5.htm > (August 7, 2006).

20. Kembrew McLeod, *Owning Culture: Authorship, Ownership, and Intellectual Property Law* (New York: P. Lang, 2001), p. 78.

21. Joanna Demers, *Steal This Music: How Intellectual Property Law Affects Musical Creativity* (n.p.: University of Georgia Press, 2006), p. 95.

22. Demers, p. 90.

23. McLeod, p. 89.

24. Ibid, p. 88.

25. Butler, p. 152.

26. Fisher, p. 41.

27. Tomas A. Lipinski, *The Complete Copyright Liability Handbook for Librarians and Educators* (New York: Neal-Schuman Publishers, 2006), p. 98.

Chapter 8 The Fair Use of Video, Computer Software, and Other Media

1. J. Michael Straczynski, *The Complete Book of Scriptwriting* (Cincinnati, Ohio: Writer's Digest Books, 1996), p. v.

2. Straczynski, p. 56.

3. Richard Stim, *Getting Permission: How to License and Clear Copyrighted Materials Online and Off,* 2nd edition (Berkeley, CA: Nolo 2004), p. 5/22.

4. Eric Bangeman, "YouTube, Google Videos Latest Targets of RIAA's Wrath," June 5, 2006, < http://arstechnica.com/news.ars/post/20060615-7065.html > (August 28, 2006).

5. William W. Fisher III, *Promises to Keep: Technology, Law, and the Future of Entertainment* (Stanford, CA: Stanford Law and Politics, 2004), p. 63.

6. Eugene Volokh and Brett McDonnell, "Freedom of Speech and Appellate and Summary Judgement Review in Copyright Cases," 1998, < http://www.law.ucla.edu/volokh/copyrev.htm > (August 8, 2006).

7. Fisher, p. 62.

8. Rebecca P. Butler, *Copyright for Teachers and Librarians* (New York: Neal-Schuman Publishers, 2004), p. 110.

9. James A. Martin, "Copying Video to a Handheld," April 20, 2006, < http://www.pcworld.com/article/125344-1/article.html > (August 6, 2006).

10. Jon L. Jacobi, "Can you legally copy DVDs?", April 6, 2004, < http://reviews.cnet.com/4520-3513_7-5128652.html > (August 6, 2006).

11. Butler, p. 120.

12. Dan Tynan, "Hollywood vs. Your PC: Round 2: Digital TV Behind the Gates," January 31, 2006), < http://www.pcworld.com/article/id,124164/article.html > (August 8, 2006).

13. Scott Thompson, "Studies show drop in illegal downloading," *Daily Universe,* via U-Wire, April 25, 2006.

14. "Hollywood steps up piracy fight," December 14, 2004, < http://money.cnn.com/2004/12/14/news/fortune500/piracy/ > (August 6, 2006).

15. Jenny Mayo, "MPAA sues grandfather over grandson's illegal download of four movies," 11/17/2005, < http://www.econoculture.com/m/index.php?option = com_content&task = view&id = 149&Itemid = 45 >.

16. Butler, p. 171.

17. "Introduction to Internet Research: Glossary of Terminology," August 1, 2002, < http://faculty.valencia.cc.fl.us/jdelisle/ lis2004/glossary.htm > (August 8, 2006).

18. Tomas A. Lipinski, *The Complete Copyright Liability Handbook for Librarians and Educators* (New York: Neal-Schuman Publishers, 2006), p. 287.

19. Kevin Savetz, "Avoiding Pirated Software," c. 1998–2006), < http://www.vendio.com/service/tipsandtactics/ buy-software.html > (August 8, 2006).

20. Gretchen McCord Hoffmann, *Copyright in Cyberspace 2: Questions and Answers for Librarians* (New York: Neal-Schuman, 2005), p. 101.

21. Kim Zetter, "Kazaa Delivers More than Tunes," January 11, 2004, < http://www.wired.com/news/business/ 0,1367,61852,00.html > (August 8, 2006).

22. R. Craig Peterson, "The Dangers of P2P File Sharing and Business Liability," *Mainstream Security Services,* c. 2002–2003, < http://www.mainstream.net/security_howto/dangers_ of_p2p_file_sharing.shtml > (August 8, 2006).

Chapter 9 Permissions

1. Stanford University Libraries, "Copyright and Fair Use—What Is Fair Use?," c. 2004, < http://fairuse.stanford.edu/Copyright _and_Fair_Use_Overview/chapter9/9-a.html > (July 27, 2006).

2. Stanford University Libraries, "Copyright and Fair Use— Website Permissions," c. 2004, < http://fairuse.stanford.edu/ Copyright_and_Fair_Use_Overview/chapter6/index.html > (July 27, 2006).

3. David Loundy, "Authors Waging Fight in Brave New World," *Chicago Law Bulletin,* March 7, 1996, < www.loundy.com/ CDLB/Electronic_Rights.html > (July 27, 2006).

4. Lloyd L. Rich, "Protection of Fictional Characters," *PubLaw,* c. 1998, < http://www.publaw.com/fiction.html > (July 27, 2006).

5. Jassin, p. 139.

6. *The New York Times,* Welcome to the Rights and Permissions FAQ, c. 2005, < http://www.nytimes.com/ref/membercenter/ help/permission.html > (July 27, 2006).

7. Washington State University, Music and Copyright, n.d., < http://publishing.wsu.edu/copyright/music_copyright/ > (July 27, 2006).

Chapter Notes

8. Copyright Clearance Center, "Overview of Copyright Law," c. 1995–2006, < http://www.copyright.com/ccc/do/viewPage? pageCode = cr10-n > (July 27, 2006).

Chapter 10 How to Protect Your Own Rights

1. University of Toronto—Computer Science Department, "How to Avoid Plagiarism," updated October 14, 2003, < http://www. cs.toronto.edu/ ~ fpitt/plagiarism.html > (July 24, 2006).

2. Gayla Almond, Cameron University Department of Psychology and Human Ecology, "Plagiarism Statement," c. 1998, < http://www.cameron.edu/ ~ beckyp/Plagiarism. html > (August 12, 2006).

3. PBS, "It's My Life: School: Cheating: Take Action!," c. 2005, < http://pbskids.org/itsmylife/school/cheating/article6.html > (August 12, 2006).

4. U.S. Copyright Office, "What Does Copyright Protect? (FAQ)" revised July 10, 2006). < http://www.copyright.gov/help/faq/ faq-protect.html > (July 26, 2006).

5. Thomas G. Field, Jr., "Copyright for Computer Authors," modified December 7, 2002, < http://www.piercelaw.edu/ tfield/copysof.htm > (July 15, 2006).

6. U.S. Copyright Office, Home Page < http://www.copyright.gov/ > (August 12, 2006).

7. About, Inc., *Copyright on the Web,* c. 2006, < http://webdesign. about.com/od/copyright/a/aa081700a.htm > (July 24, 2006).

8. Richard Keyt, "Remedies for Web Site Copyright Infringement, July 10, 2006, < www.keytlaw.com/Copyrights/cheese.htm > (July 24, 2006).

Glossary

bibliography—A general list of sources that appears at the end of a paper or a book.

citation—A note that identifies the original source of information included in a research paper, book, or other publication. A citation includes the name of the author, the title of the source, and the source's publication information.

common knowledge—Well-established facts that are known by most people.

copyright—The legal right granted to a creator to control the use of his or her work.

copyright infringement—Unlawful use or reproduction of material protected by copyright.

Creative Commons license—A special license that allows someone to use copyrighted materials.

derivative work—A new work that is based on and draws substantially from the ideas of an earlier work.

download—To copy a file onto your computer from an outside source, such as another computer or the Internet.

endnote—A citation note placed at the end of a paper or book that identifies the work or source used for the section of text marked by the endnote's reference number.

footnote—A citation note placed at the bottom of a page that identifies the work or source used for the section of text marked by the footnote's reference number.

honor code—A set of rules about behavior that students are expected to follow.

infringement—An act that disregards a right.

paraphrase—To reword or restate something in your own words that someone else has written or said.

parody—A work that makes fun of something.

patent—A document that protects the rights of an inventor, granting him or her the sole right for a period of time to make and sell the invention.

permission—The act of asking for or receiving the right to use material that belongs to someone else.

plagiarism—Copying material without giving proper credit.

public domain—Material that is no longer copyrighted, or that has never been copyrighted.

quote—To repeat someone's words exactly.

summary—A presentation of material in a condensed or shortened form.

trademarks—Symbols and names used by companies to distinguish their products from similar products produced by other companies.

Further Reading

Books

Gordon, Sherri Mabry. *Downloading Copyrighted Stuff from the Internet: Stealing or Fair Use?* Berkeley Heights, NJ: Enslow Publishers, Inc., 2005.

Orr, Tamra. *Extraordinary Research Projects.* Danbury, CT: Franklin Watts, 2006.

Robson, Colin. *How to Do a Research Project.* London: Blackwell, 2007.

Strausser, Jeffrey. *Painless Writing.* Hauppauge, NY: Barron's, 2001.

Internet Addresses

Internet Public Library's TeenSpace
A+ Research and Writing site
http://www.ipl.org/div/aplus/

The Learning Center at Plagiarism.org
http://www.plagiarism.org/learning_center/home.html

A Research Guide for Students
http://www.aresearchguide.com

Index